EDOARDO BONECHI

FLORENCE

A COMPLETE GUIDE FOR VISITING THE CITY

BONECHI - EDIZIONI « IL TURISMO » - FLORENCE
5, Via dei Rustici

«MERCURIO» SERIES
OF BONECHI GUIDE

Impianto Offset
eseguito dalla ditta « LA FOTOLITOGRAFIA »
FIRENZE

Have a Happy Stay in Florence!

It is my belief that all those who visit a city for the first time wish to gain, in little time and money, as accurate impressions as possible to keep as souvenirs. However, this is not a simple thing to do in those rare centres which — like Florence — have given shape to ages, refined or completed the history of the world, through works expressed in an atmosphere of almost miraculous continuity and perfection. In places such as Florence it does not suffice to give a panoramic glance, but it is indispensable to look analytically and to classify the works of art. Only thus can one fully appreciate its beauty and proportions.

It is with this book, reduced in size but containing all essential facts and comments concerning Florence, that I wish to introduce you to this city. It is here where, from the XII century until late in the Renaissance and to our day, art and science have produced its greatest geniuses.

In its chiaroscuri which reveal at each instant manifestations and phenomena that are unique in power and character Florence presents itself to you with all its unmistakable personality. This city is rendered all the more suggestive by its splendid lights and sweet shades which will be described in this book also containing its lights and shades.

Hoping to be useful to you through this book, I wish to express a most cordial welcome to Florence. Have a good time!

THE EDITOR

A FEW HISTORICAL HINTS ON THE CITY OF FLORENCE

The origins of Florence go back to the period of the Etruscans when Fiesole an important city of Etruria built on top of a hill, dominated the valley. A group of its inhabitants went down the banks of the river to give life to a village, even if a modest one, but destined to develop because of a favorable position. This position was, however, an easy prey for ennemies and invaders. As a matter of fact the Romans themselves put their tends there and founded a colony with the name of Florence, which means « destined to flourish ».

Since the first century A.B. this Roman Municipality affirms itself acquiring later a preeminent position among the cities of Tuscia, especially beginning from the III century A.D. as we see in the « Corrector Italiae ». It survived the most obscure periods of the Middle Ages to resurrect slowly during the period of Carolingian emperors, and becoming one of the most important centres in the peninsula, from a cultural point of view also. At first a feud of Tuscan Marquises, among whom are remembered Ugo and Matilde, Florence gained from the XI an ever-increasing autonomy: in 1115, at the end of fights agains the clergy and the founders of the region, the Florentine Commune is practically constituted. Ten years later the new state suppressed rival Fiesole. Soon at the interior of the city, surrounded with new walls, appear the first contrasts between the owners of fiefs and the working classes, organized in Corporations.

The contrasts take the form of two factions: the Guelfs and the Ghibellines. The former are partisans of the pope, the latter of the Emperor. Florence has, however, a prevalence of Guelfs. It was these who from the end of the XIII century divided themselves into two factions: the whites and the blacks. The black party, supported by the Pontiff, in 1303 sends to exile the white party and among these Dante Alighieri is the « wandering Ghibelline ».

In the meantime Florence increased her power by fighting her rivals: Pistoia, Arezzo, Volterra, Siena. Culturally and economically also between the end of the thirteenth and the fourteenth century Florence was becoming one of Italy's most important centres. It is the age of Dante and Giotto, of the great companies of Bankers and Merchants, of the great industry of wool and silk. In the first decennia of the .XIV century Florence goes through several political and economic experiences: first in the struggle against the last Ghibellines, then during the Signorie of Carlo di Calabria and Gualtieri di Brienne the Duke of Athens (1343).

The year 1348 marks the period of the plague, which is described by Boccaccio. The last decennia of the fourteenth century see ever-growing contrasts between the « fat people », that is, the rich bourgeoisie which leads the state through the Major Arts and the « minor people ».

The fight reaches its climax in the « tumult of Ciompi » (1378), the humble workers of the Arte della Lana, through which the lower stratum of the citizenry obtain representation. Soon enough, hower, the oligarchy, led by the Albizzi, had the best of the situation. In the meantime the Medici family, leaning on the people, was gaining more and more political influence.

In a short time the Signoria was constitued, even though preserving its Republican appearances. To the founder of the Medici Signoria Cosimo the Elder, succeeded Lorenzo later called Ma-

LOGGIA DEL BIGALLO. - Florence in 1300.
(Detail of the fresco « The Madonna of Mercy »).

gnifico, an acute politician and a great man. The century which culminates in the Signoria of Magnifico is one of the most enlightened in Florentine history, especially in the cultural and artistic fields: it is the age of Humanism which has in Florence its centre.

For a few more years the city remained a free Republic: between the end of the fifteeth century and the beginning of the sixteenth century, after the expulsion of Piero the successor of Lorenzo. This glorious period is dominated by the figure of Girolamo Savonarola. Once the Medici returned, Florence was under their Signoria until 1527, when a new insurrection gave once again the much-desired Republican government to the city.

The Medicis, however, supported by the Emperor and the Pope came back after a very long siege (1530). Even during the restless political life, the years between the end of the fifteenth century and the first decennia of the sixteenth century are rich of the greatest personalities in the artistic and literary fields (Michelangelo, Machiavelli, Guicciardini). In 1569 Cosimo de' Medici, the head of the city, was given the title of Grand Duke which he passed to is successors until the extinction of the Giangastone Dynasty, (1737). The successors were the Lorenas who made the Grand Duchy, except for the period of the domination of Napoleon (1799-1814), until the reunion of Florence and Tuscany with Italy (1859).

Finally Florence wa the capital of Italy from 1865 to 1871.

INDEX OF ITINERARIES

FIRST ITINERARY . . . . Page 16
Piazza del Duomo (Baptistery; Giotto's Bell-Tower; Loggia del Bigallo; Cathedral of Santa Maria del Fiore; Opera del Duomo Museum) - Medici - Riccardi Palace (Medici Museum) - Piazza San Lorenzo (Church of San Lorenzo; Laurenziana Library; Medici Chapels).

SECOND ITINERARY . . . . Page 54
Piazza del Duomo - Via dei Calzaiuoli - Church of Orsanmichele - Piazza della Signoria (Loggia della Signoria; Palazzo Vecchio) - Uffizi Square (Uffizi Gallery).

THIRD ITINERARY . . . . Page 108
Piazza della Repubblica - Loggia del Mercato Nuovo (New Market) - Via Por Santa Maria - Ponte Vecchio - Via Guicciardini - Pitti Square (Pitti Palace; Palatine Gallery; Gallery of Modern Art; Royal Apartments; Museum of the Historical Carriages; Silver Museum; Boboli Garden) - Via Romana - Via Maggio - Church of Santo Spirito - Church of Santa Maria del Carmine (Brancacci Chapel).

FOURTH ITINERARY . . . . Page 137
Piazza del Duomo - Via dei Cerretani - Via Tornabuoni - Strozzi Palace - Piazza Santa Trinita (Church of Santa Trinita; Church of the Apostles) - Santa Trinita Bridge - Lungarno Corsini (Corsini Gallery) - Cascine Park - Piazza and Church of Ognissanti - Piazza Santa Maria Novella (Church and Cloister of Santa Maria Novella.

FIFTH ITINERARY . . . . Page 152
Piazza del Duomo - Via Cavour - Cenacolo di Sant'Apollonia - Cloister of Scalzo - Piazza San Marco (Church of San Marco; Museum of San Marco or of Angelico) - Gallery of the Academy - Piazza SS. Annunziata (Church of SS. Annunziata; Spedale degli Innocenti; Archaeological Museum) - Synagogue - Convent of Santa Maria Maddalena de' Pazzi - Church of Sait Ambrose

SIXTH ITINERARY . . . . Page 168
Piazza del Duomo - Via del Proconsolo - Dante's Home - Piazza Santa Croce (Church of Santa Croce; Pazzi Chapel; Museum of the Opera of Santa Croce) - Horne Museum - Bardini Museum.

SEVENTH ITINERARY . . . . Page 189
Viale dei Colli - Piazzale Michelangelo - Church of San Miniato al Monte - Via San Leonardo - Forte Belvedere.

MUSEO STIBBERT . . . . Page 197

CARTHUSIAN MONASTERY (of Val d'Ema) . . Page 204

FIESOLE .. . . Page 199

SUBJECT INDEX

Museums, Galleries, Churches, Palaces, Monuments, etc.

	Page
Boboli Gardens	130
Bridge of Santa Trinita	144
Campanile of Giotto	26
Cascine	144
Cenacolo di Sant'Apollonia	152
CHAPELS:	
- Brancacci	134
- Medici	49
- Pazzi	186
- Rucellai	138
Chiostro dello Scalzo	152
CHURCHES:	
- Badia	177
- Baptistery	16
- Cathedral (S. Maria del Fiore)	28
- Ognissanti	146
- Orsanmichele	54
- San Felice	131
- San Gaetano	136
- San Lorenzo	48
- San Marco	153
- San Miniato al Monte	192
- San Salvatore al Monte	190
- Santa Croce	178
- Santa Felicita	110
- Santa Maria al Carmine	134
- Santa Maria Maggiore	137
- Santa Maria Novella	147
- Santa Trinita	142
- SS. Annunziata	164
- SS. Apostoli	140
- Santo Spirito	132
Cloister of San Domenico	158
» of S. Maria Novella	150
» of Sant'Antonino	156
Forte Belvedere (Fortress)	194
Fresco by Perugino (S. Maria Maddalena de' Pazzi)	167
GALLERIES:	
- Academy	158
- Arte Moderna (Modern Art)	112
- Corsini	144
- Innocenti (degli)	164
- Palatine	112
- Uffizi	78
House of Dante	170
Laurentian Library	49
LOGGIAS:	
- Bigallo	28
- Mercato Nuovo (New Market)	108
- Rucellai	138
- Signoria (della)	63
Lungarno Corsini	144
Medici Chapels	49
MUSEUMS:	
- Anthropology and Ethnology	170
- Archaeological	166
- Bardini	188
- Buonarroti	178
- Cathedral (Opera del Duomo)	39
- Horne	188
- Mediceo	44
- National (Bargello)	171
- Precious Stones	126
- San Marco	153
- Santa Croce	188
- Stibbert	197
PALACES:	
- Altoviti	140
- Antella (dell')	178
- Antinori	137
- Bargello	170
- Bartolini-Salimbeni	140
- Cocchi Serristori	178
- Corsi	137
- Corsini	144
- Davanzati	108
- Gianfigliazzi	140
- Gondi	170
- Guicciardini	110
- Lardarel	137
- Medici-Riccardi	44
- Minerbetti	140
- Nonfinito	168
- Parte Guelfa	108
- Pazzi Quaratesi	170
- Pitti	110
- Rucellai	138
- Signoria (Palazzo Vecchio)	66
- Spini-Ferroni	140
- Strozzi	138
- Viviani già della Robia	137
PIAZZE (Squares):	
- Antinori	137
- Duomo (del)	16
- Ognissanti	146
- Repubblica (della)	108
- San Firenze	170
- San Lorenzo	48
- San Marco	153
- Santa Croce	178
- Santa Maria Novella	147
- Santa Trinita	140
- SS. Annunziata	164
- Signoria (della)	59
Piazzale degli Uffizi	77
Piazzale Michelangelo	190
Ponte Vecchio	109
Royal Apartments	126
Synagogue	167
Spedale of the Innocenti	164
Viale dei Colli	189
VIE (Streets):	
- Calimala	108
- Calzaiuoli (dei)	54
- Cerretani	131
- Guicciardini	110
- Maggio	131
- Martelli	44
- Proconsolo (del)	168
- San Leonardo	194
- Tornabuoni	137
CERTOSA DEL GALLUZZO	204
FIESOLE	199

FLORENTINE PAINTING

In the thirteenth century those artists who were working in Florence received much influence from Byzantine art and even the decoration of the dome of the Baptistery of Saint John, which goes back to this period, has a Byzantine appearance. The mosaic decoration was the work of Roman and Venetian artists and without a doubt the contact of these artists with local elements contributed to the formation of a Florentine school which has in Cimabue its first painter (1240-1302). It seems that he has also worked in the mosaics of the Baptistery; in any event, he knew how to free himself brom Byzantine influence and direct painting towards a more human and realistic conception. Perhaps his tentative of reform would have been in vain had he not found in his disciple Giotto di Bondone the accomplisher of his postulates. Giotto is thus to be considered the true innovator of Florentine painting; not only, but of all the painting of the age.

Giotto (1266-1336), taking advantage of the school of Cimabue and of the Roman School of Cavallini, frees himself from all traces of Byzantine influence in order to create an art which adheres fully to reality, which is powerfully human, treated according to a volumetric conception of the masses and contained within a certain rythm, which is incisive and harmonious at the same time. It is enough to observe his Madonna at the Uffizi Gallery and the frescos in Santa Croce. A whole group of painters were under the influence of Giotto who worked in several Italian cities. Scholars who stayed by the great master and who helped him were Giottino (XIV century) identified as Maso di Banco, the author of the frescos of San Silvestro in Santa Croce and Taddeo Gaddi (1300-66) who in the frescos of the Baroncelli Chapel in Santa Croce reveals a certain influence from the Senese school where the best artists were Duccio di Boninsegna (1255-1318) operating around 1285 in Florence, Pietro Lorenzetti, (1280-1348), Ambrogio Lorenzetti (1348 d.) and the lyrical Simone Martini (1285-1344) who also came to work in Florence. The Florentine artists in whom we find these two tendencies mixed, the one of Giotto and the other from the Senese, were Bernardo Daddi (active between 1320 and 1380) as we can see in the frescos of San Lorenzo and Santo Stefano in Santa Croce, Nardo with his brother Andrea Orcagna (1308-68 - Strozzi Chapel in Santa Maria Novella), while Giovanni da Milano (active in Florence from 1350) also a pupil of Giotto preserved in the frescos of the Rinuccini chapel in Santa Croce the character of the Lombard school thus having an influence in the pleasing and decorative eclectism of Andrea Bonaiuti called Andrea da Firenze (1333-92 — the Spaniard's Chapel in the cloisters of Santa Maria Novella), by Agnolo Gaddi (1333-96 — choir of Santa Croce) and Spinello Aretino (1333-1410 — sacresty of San Miniato on the Hill).

With the fifteenth century Florence has a leadership in painting: Lorenzo Monaco (1370-1425), an exquisite representative of the late Gothic; Gentile da Fabriano (1370-1428) tied to an international Gothic (Adoration of the Magi, at the Uffizi); Masolino da Panicale (1384-1447 — frescos in the Brancacci Chapel in the church of Santa Maria del Carmine). These artists brought a reflection of international art in Florentine painting, until Tommaso Guidi di Ser Giovanni called Masaccio (1401-28 or 29) frees himself from any Gothic traces and returns to the frankness and plasticity of Giotto by making also use of Donatello's ideas and those of Brunelleschi, thus creating the miracle which is the Brancacci Chapel in the Church of Carmine. His new style influenced almost all painters of the epoch beginning from his very maestro Masolino da Panicale. In the perspective followed him Paolo Uccello (1397-1475 — frescos of the Green Cloister in Santa Maria Novella) while Andrea del Castagno (1423-57 — frescos in the supper-room of Saint Apollonia) developped the plasticity of the figure. At the same time Father Giovanni from Fiesole called Beato Angelico (1387-1455) made his new conquests of chromatic and celestial harmonies (Saint Mark Museum) and Filippo Lippi (1405-69) forms himself on him adhering, however, to a more earthly language and coming closer to Masaccio (Uffizi Gallery, Pitty Gallery and church of San Lorenzo). His apprentice and helper is Benozzo Gozzoli (1420-98) an interesting and most pleasing narrator of sacred legends (chapel of th Magi in the Medici-Riccardi Palace).

In the seconf half of the XV century we find Alessio Baldovinetti (1425-99), the pupil of Andrea del Castagno (Uffizi Gallery, church of Saint Ambrose, SS. Annunziata and San Miniato); Piero (1443-96) and above all his brother Antonio del Pollaiolo (1432-98) who were also goldsmiths and sculptors (Uffizi Gallery, San Miniato and the Bardini Museum); Andrea di Cione called Verrocchio (1435-88 also a goldsmith and sculptor (Baptism of Christ, in the Uffizi) who also had Leonardo in his workshop; Domenico Bigordi called Ghirlandaio (1449-94) a festive narrator of sacred stories (church of Santa Maria Novella and Sassetti chapel in Santa Trinita); Alessandro Filipepi called Botticelli (1445-1510), a pupil of Lippi who was formed by Verrocchio and Pollaiolo, but isolated and the creator of a style all his own, particularly Florentine, in which prevails rythm and the great lyrism; Filippino Lippi (1457-1504), the disciple and companion of Botticelli, who also felt the inbuence of his style. These artists take us to the true representatives of the « Golden Age », to Leonardo da Vinci (1452-1519) the creator of a new mysterious chiaroscuro. By him Florence has only works of the first period (Uffizi Gallery). To Fra Bartolomeo della Porta (1475-1517) who after the Venetian stay acquires a better sense of colour, to Michelangelo Buonarroti (1475-1564) who has left only the big tondo of the Holy Family which is at the Uffizi Gallery, to Raffaello Sanzio (1483-1520) who, after Umbria, made Florence his adopted country (Uffizi Gallery and Pitti Gallery), to Andrea di Agnolo called Andrea del Sarto (1468-1531) who reveals a special manner of treating form and colour (church of SS. Annunziata, Scalzo Cloister, San Salvi, Uffizi Gallery) and who has followers such as Iacopo Carrucci called Pontormo (1494-1557), a great designer and colourist (fresco of the villa of Poggio at Caiano), Giovambattista di Iacopo called Rosso Fiorentino (1495-1540), Francesco Bigi called Franciabigio (1482-1525) and Francesco Ubertini called Bacchiacca (1490-1557).

The great art of these artists who sought perfection in forms brought to an « academic mannerism » which influenced a little everyone from Agnolo Allori called Bronzino (1503-72) and Francesco de' Rossi called Cecchino Salviati (1510-63) to Giorgio Vasari (1511-74) whose great frescos are found in the Palazzo Vecchio. In the last part of the century Santi di Tito (1538-1603) followed again Fra Bartolomeo and Andrea del Sarto and Bernardino Poccetti (1548-1612) distinguished himself for his decorative gifts.

Between the sixteenth and the seventeenth century we have Ludovico Cardi called Cigoli (1559-1613), Alessandro Allori (1535-1607), Francesco Morandini called Poppi, Empoli, Domenico Cresti called Passignano (1560-1638) and in the middle of the seventeenth century the school of Matteo Rosselli (1578-1650), Francesco Furini (1600-46), Lorenzo Lippi, Iacopo Vignali the maestro of Carlo Dolci and Giovanni Mannozzi called Giovanni da San Giovanni (1592-1636), who decorated the hall of the Silver Museum in the Pitti Palace.

Florentine painting does not have much merit in the following period until, after the neo-classical parenthesis at the beginning of the XIX century. Leader of this movement was Pietro Benvenuti (1761-1844), a follower of David, and after the reaction to this movement due to Giuseppe Bezzuoli, Luigi Mussini, Antonio Ciseri, Pollastrini, Puccinelli and Stefano Ussi, we meet the revolutionary movement which has its centre in the « Caffè Michelangelo » and which begins around 1850. The artists that took part in it were called « macchiaioli » because they sought to represent truth by means of a « macchia » (stain) where the details of figures and things were understood.

A revolutionary movement which goes together with the impressionist movement and has a character all its own. The first group of « macchiaioli » were Giovanni Fattori, Telemaco Signorini, Silvestro Lega, Raffaello Sernesi, Giuseppe Abbati, Serafino de' Tivoli, Odoardo Borrani, Cristiano Banti, Vito d'Ancona and Adriano Cecioni. The most famous are Giovanni Fattori (1825-1908), Silvestro Lega (1826-95) and Telemaco Signorini (1835-1901). In the last decennia of the XIX century the Florentine School was represented by the followers of the « macchiaioli » among whom Egisto Ferroni, Niccolò Cannicci, Francesco Gioli and Cesare Ciani. The works of the « macchiaioli » and of « post-macchiaioli » are found in the Gallery of Modern Art in the Pitti Palace.

SCULPTURE IN FLORENCE

Throughout the Renaissance Florence is the leader in sculpture. In the Romanesque period does not exist in Florence a school of its own, while Pisa had Nicola Pisano who had already brought new life to this art, continued later by his son Giovanni Pisano. In Florence, we find at the beginning of the Gothic period Arnolfo di Cambio (1232-1302), a pupil and collaborator of Nicola Pisano and who introduced motifs of the Pisan School in the sculptures for the facade of the cathedral.

Giotto di Bondone also (1266-1336), who had been the architect of the belltower, designed and made part of the plastic decoration of the building, but the real founder of the Florentine School is Andrea da Pontedera called Andrea Pisano (1270-1348). In 1330 he began the doors of the Baptistery of Florence and in 1337 he succeeded Giotto in the construction of the bell tower by decorating it with bas-reliefs on the various activities of human labour: these are among the most beautiful sculptures in the century even if the drawings are attributed to Giotto.

The third great artist is Andrea di Cione called Orcagna (1308-68), a painter, sculptor, architect and poet; a true precursor of the universal artists of the following century. A pupil of Giotto and Andrea Pisano he knew how to combine the two tendencies and expressed himself in a style which knows force and grace. His great work is the tabernacle in the church of Orsanmichele begun in 1349 and finished ten years later. The style of the work is Gothic, but the sculptures are Tuscan.

At the beginning of the fifteenth century Lorenzo Ghiberti (1378-1455), the creator of the door of the Baptistery called « the door of Paradise », reveals the grandeur of his genius by bringing a perspective and pictorial vision of nature in the bas-relief. The cornice of the doors made by him, as well as that for the door by Andrea Pisano, are a wonder of verist decoration. In the external tabernacles of the church of Orsanmichele, are also found three statues made by Ghiberti. Nanni di Banco also (1380-1421), was the author of Saint Filippo and other statues in the church of Orsanmichele, of San Luca in the tribune of

San Zanobi in the cathedral, and of a bas-relief placed above the door of the Mandorla (almond) in the same cathedral, belongs to the first part of the fifteenth century. But the central figure of this period is Donato di Nicolò di Betto de' Bardi called Donatello (1386-1466) who revolutionizes the whole field of sculpture by giving it a naturalistic characteristics and gives a new interpretation of reality adherent to the single objecte, passing through the multiplicity of expressions and characters (National Museum, Baptistery, Cathedral, the Opera del Duomo Museum) and giving a new interpretation also to the bas-relief lito which takes from him the name of « stiacciato »; that is to say, considered with very little relief.

Donatello had his followers: Antonio Rossellino (1427-79) and his brother Bernardo Rossellino (1409-64) with the works which are found in the church of Santa Croce in the National Museum and in the church of Santa Maria Novella; Desiderio da Settignano (1428-64) who died as a very young man and was the leader of a wonderful school of marble, leaving there heads of virgins, portraits of women and children of a sweetness veiled with sadness and of great sentiment; Benedetto da Maiano (1442-97) who followed the art of Bernardo and Antonio Rossellino (church of Santa Croce, church of Santa Maria Novella, Cathedral, National Museum); Luca della Robbia (1400-82) finds in his glazed earthenwares the style to manifest the beauty and vivacity of his models (gallery in the museum of the Opera del Duomo, where adolescents dance, play and sing with joy and spontaneity): many works by him are also found in the National Museum and his artistic heredity passes to his nephew Andrea della Robbia (1435-1528) and to five of his sons, of whom the most notable is Giovanni (1460-1529), the author of the frieze and the medallions of the Hospital of Ceppo in Pistoia.

Two personalities stand out in the middle of the fifteenth century. They are Andrea di Cione called Verrocchio (1435-88) and Antonio del Pollaiolo (1429-98): both goldsmiths loved realism and bronze. Andrea del Verrocchio was a great researcher and investigator of new things and was the forerunner of his pupil Leonardo (National Museum, Palazzo Vecchio, Orsanmichele); Antonio del Pollaiolo is notable for his proud realism (National Museum). These two artists were also painters.

We thus reach the sixteenth century dominated fully by the gigantic figure of Michelangelo Buonarroti (1475-1564) who interpreted powerfully the drama of humanity and impressed with his style and genius all the sculpture of the following period (Gallery of the Academy, Palazzo Vecchio, National Museum, Michelangiolo's House).

Among Florentine sculptors who felt more strongly the influence of Michelangelo were Baccio Bandinelli (1488-1560) and Bartolomeo Ammannati (1511-92), an architect of merit but an imitator of the forms of Michelangelo as a sculptor. Ammannati's imitation is without the spirit of the « Titan » (see the Neptune of the fountain of Piazza della Signoria).

In the middle of the sixteenth century we find a unique kind of artist: Benvenuto Cellini (1500-71). He was and remained essentially a goldsmith and brought to sculpture the preciousness of his profession; we only have to look at his most famous work of sculpture which is « Perseus » under the Loggia of Signoria. He dominates in the field of goldsmith's trade and is also the author of beautiful medals.

The last great sculptor of the Renaissance is Jean Boulogne called Giambologna, born in Flanders but an Italian by adoption (1529-1608). He came to Italy in 1551, first in Rome and then in Florence where he settled. Even though he felt the great lesson of Michelangelo, he reveals his strong personality which manifests

UFFIZI GALLERY. - « Venus of the Medicis ».
(Hellenistic ar to the III century B. C.).

itself in the impetuosity of movements combined with a certain harmonius, rythmic composition (Loggia of Signoria, National Museum).

Florentine sculptors, influenced by Michelangelo, revealed a certain eclectism, among whom Nicolò Pericoli called Tribolo (1500-58) who made the fountain of Hercules and Anteo a Castello; Lorenzo di Lodovico or Lorenzetto (1489-1541); Simone Mosca (1492-1553) who was above all a decorator.

In the seventeenth and eighteenth centuries sculpture declined in Florence exercised by the disciples of Giambologna: Pietro Tacca (1577-1640), Pietro Francavilla (1553-1615), Giovan Battista Caccini (1556-1613). In the nineteenth century the Tuscan School fought the new mannerism deriving from Canova and returned to the study of nature. His disciple was Giovanni Dupré (1817-82).

ARCHITECTURE IN FLORENCE

Very little remains from the Roman period: foundations of Campidoglio, Praetorium, Theatre, Baths and various fragments are kept in the Archaeological Museum. In the XI century, with the coming of the new Romanesque architecture, Florence takes part by building churches such as the Baptistery, San Miniato, the Badia from Fiesole, San Salvatore, SS. Apostles and Iacopo on the Arno. The Gothic element, brought at the middle of the XIII century with the construction of the church of Badia a Settimo, felt very much the influence of local elements; for this reason the Florentine Gothc differs from that of other countries and has a characteristic all its own. Construction of this period are Santa Maria Novella, Santa Croce, Santa Trinita and Santa Maria Maggiore, all buildings of sacred character. But towards the end of the thirteenth century and the beginning of the fourteenth century an interest for civil construction appears and we see the Palace of the Podestà, the Signoria Palace, the Loggia dei Signori, the Loggia del Bigallo and luxurious palaces such as the Davanzati,, Feroni, Capponi, Bardi and numerous others. In the thirteenth century the great genius of Arnolfo di Cambio (1232-1302) is the dominat figure among Italian architects. He was able to give a severe noble elegance to its buildings such as we can see in Santa Maria del Fiore, Palazzo Vecchio, Santa Croce and Orsanmichele. To him succeeded architects who felt the Gothic influence beginning from Giotto (1266-1336) who began the Cathedral, to Francesco Talenti (d. 1380), the one who continued the Cathedral and the bell tower, to Benci di Cione (d. 1388), the builder of the church of San Carlo, of the couryard and of the staircase in the palace of the Podestà (Bargello), of the Loggia of Signoria, and Orsanmichele (in part). The latter was finished by Simone Talenti.

The initiator and leader of architecture in the Renaissance was Filippo Brunelleschi (1377-1446) who reacted to each influence from the Gothic by creating a classic style all his own, by uniting a clear stone to plaster in a simplicity of harmonious motifs (hall of the Parte Guelfa Palace, Old Sacresty of San Lorenzo, Innocenti Hospital, the Pazzi Chapel in the cloister of Santa Croce and the Pitti Palace). He also gave to Santa Maria del Fiore the famous dome; which was the greatest undertaking in his life.

One of Brunelleschi's pupils is Michelozzo (1392-1472) whose most important work is the Medici Palace, enlarged in the seven teenth century.

He also built the convent of San Marco, the chapel of the Medici in the church of SS. Annunziata and the villas of Careggi and Cafaggiolo.

Other contemporary architects are successors of Brunelleschi; they felt the influence of his art and returned to the spirit and forms of classical architecture, with constructions of exquisite balance which is the main feature of Florentine art. For example, Giuliano Giamberti called Giuliano da Sangallo (1445-1516 - Santa Maria Maddalena de' Pazzi, sacresty and vestibule of Santo Spirito); Simone del Pollaiolo called Cronaca (1454-1508 San Salvatore al Monte); Giuliano da Maiano (1432-90 - Pazzi-Quarantesi Palace); Benedetto da Maiano (1442-97 - Strozzi Palace).

Leon Battista Alberti is quite far from Brunelleschi's style. This artist, the precursor of architects of the sixteenth century was the innovator of new motifs and the true type of universal artist like, after him, Leonardo da Vinci. A humanist, man of letters and poet, sculptor and author of scientific treatises, Leon Battista Alberti was above all an architect. His masterpiece is the Rucellai Palace where he fragmented the windows with pillars, a motif which was later repeated by the architects of the century. He also created the facade of Santa Maria Novella and the tribune of the church of SS. Annunziata.

With the sixteenth century is interrupted the tradition of Brunelleschi. Baccio Baglioni called Baccio d'Agnolo (1462-1543) creates the new type of elegant construction which will be followed throughout the century. For example, Guadagni Palace, Taddei Palace, Bartolini Palace at Santa Trinita, tower of San Miniato and the bell tower of Santo Spirito. In this period Raffaello made his designs for the Pandolfini Palace in San Gallo Street, where the Florentine characteristics lose their elements.

One example of prodigious activity is Antonio da Sangallo the Elder (1455-1534), a civil and military architect who designed and planned very many buildings of many kinds among which Saint Peter's in Rome and the Farnese Palace. As a military architect we owe him the reconstruction of Castel Sant'Angelo in Rome.

Then comes the great Michelangelo Buonarrotti (1475-1564) who goes back to the Florentine and classical spirit, faithful to Brunelleschi in combining clear stone and plaster. Buonarroti built in Florence the New sacresty or Medici chapel in San Lorenzo and began also the project for the facade of the church, besides the Laurenziana Library, a bold construction of great impact. He continued his great projects in Rome where he also carried out the works in Saint Peter's.

In the meantime Giorgio Vasari (1511-74) creates the Uffizi colonnade and decorates the interior of Palazzo Vecchio, and Bartolomeo Ammannati (1511-92) builds the courtyard of the Pitti Palace and the stupendous bridge of Santa Trinita.

The Baroque (1600-1700) has in Florence few artists to represent it: Matteo Nigetti (1560-1649) builds the facade of San Gaetano and that of Ognissanti and Ferdinando Ruggeri (XVIII century) the facade of San Firenze.

Thus we reach the nineteenth century when architecture tries to take up classical and traditional motifs with Architect Giuseppe Poggi (1811-1901), the creator of the famous Piazzale Michelangelo from which a very beautiful view of the panorama of the city of Florence opens before our eyes. Little by little, however, in the confusion of styles, the engineer overshadows the architect and one can no longer speak of architectural works of art.

FIRST ITINERARY

PIAZZA DEL DUOMO (BAPTISTERY; GIOTTO'S BELL-TOWER; LOGGIA DEL BIGALLO; CATHEDRAL OF SANTA MARIA DEL FIORE; OPERA DEL DUOMO MUSEUM) - MEDICI-RICCARDI PALACE (MEDICI MUSEUM) - PIAZZA SAN LORENZO (CHURCH OF S. LORENZO; LAURENZIANA LIBRARY; MEDICI CHAPELS).

Piazza del Duomo. — With Piazza San Giovanni, which surrounds the Baptistery, constitutes the centre of the city. The religious monuments found there are: the Baptistery, the Cathedral or Santa Maria del Fiore, and Giotto's Bell-tower. These harmonize stupendously due to the polychromy of white, pink and green marbles arranged in a rigorously geometric order. Near the northern door of the Baptistery rises the COLUMN OF SAN ZANOBI, a Florentine bishop of the V cetury. This column was placed here in 1384 in memory of the Saint's miracle; namely, the sudden blooming of a dry elm tree as His corpse was passing by.

THE BAPTISTERY

It is one of Florence's most ancient buildings. Dante, who was baptized there, called it, « my beautiful San Giovanni» . Thought at first to be a V century construction, it is now believed to be a Romanesque work of the latter part of the XI century. This building rose on the remains of a paleochristian monument in the foundations of which were found remains of Roman construction. It is an example of Romanesque-tuscan architecture in an octagonal plan with colored marbles, enclosed by a double order of pillars which support. the arches. The cover of the dome is hidden by an attic (XIII century). It was consecrated to Saint John the Baptist and was the cathedral of Florence until 1128. The three entrance doors, of exceptional interest, are located in reference to the cardinal points.

The Baptistery of Saint John the Baptist.

THE BAPTISTERY. - Interior.

THE INTERIOR. — Before describing the external doors, it is advisable to visit the interior which one usually enters from the southern door. The construction, in an octagonal plan, represents two orders: the inferior one has Corynthian columns layed upon the wall; the superior one has a narrow gallery with windows. The walls are geometrically decorated in colored marbles which reveal the Romanesque-florentine style. The floor recreates the Zodiac signs as well as scenes from Oriental textiles. At the right side is located the marble baptismal font of the Pisan school of the year 1371 with six bas-reliefs, which was originally located at the centre of the building. At the left wall from the tribune, is found a statue in wood of the *magdalen*, a work by Donatello of powerful realism. At the right wall, *tomb of antepope John XXIII*, who died in Florence in 1419. This work was by Donatello and Michelozzo (1427). The triumphal arch of the apse and of the cupola are a splendor of Byzantine mosaics of the XIII century made by Venetian and Florentine artists. The mosaics of the tribune were started in 1225 by Iacopo da Torrita and represent busts of *Christ, Mary, Apostoles, and Prophets,* in the double and under-arch; the *mystic Lamb surrounded by Prophets and Patriarchs at the centre of the vault; the Madonna with Her Child* at the right an the *Enthroned Baptist* at the left.
On the right the marble angel holding the chandelier is the work of Agostino di Iacopo (1320). The mosaics in the dome (lighted up on request) were made by Venetian and Florentine artists of the second half of the XIII and the beginning of the XIV century among whom are found Cimabue, Andrea di Riccio also called Tafo and Gaddo Gaddi. On the three sides corresponding to the tribune is represented the *Final Judgement* with Christ's gigantic figure (over 9 yards high). In the first zone there are ornamental motifs; in the second *celestial hierarchies;* in the third, *history of the Genesis;* in the fourth,

BAPTISTERY. - Mosaic of the Cupola: Hell.

BAPTISTERY. - Mosaic of the Cupola: Christ in Judgment.

BAPTISTERY. — **Lorenzo Ghiberti:** « The door of Paradise ».

histories of Joseph; in the fifth, *stories of Christ;* in the sixth, *stories of the Baptist.*

SOUTHERN DOOR. — It is the most ancient door. Modelled by Andrea da Pontedera, called the Pisan, (1330-36), it was cast by the Venetian Leonardo D'Avanzo. It is divided into 28 parts which tell the *stories of Saint John the Baptist and the allegories of cardinal and theological virtues.* The door-posts are by Vittorio Ghiberti, the son of Lorenzo (1462).
The three statues in bronze on the trabeation of the door are by Vincenzo Danti (1571), and represent *John the Baptist between Salome and the executioner.* On the sides of the door are two Roman sarcophagi with funeral allegories (II-III centuries).

NORTHERN DOOR. — It is the work of Lorenzo Ghiberti (1403-24) in collaboration with Donatello, Paolo Uccello, Bernardo Ciuffagni and Bernardo Cennini. The history of this door, usually disregarded by visitors is indeed very interesting. The construction of this door was put up for competition in 1402 with the participation of some of the best artists of the time among whom are Ghiberti, Brunelleschi, Iacopo della Quercia, Nicolò Lamberti and others. The topic of the contest was an episode of the Old Testament: the sacrifice of Isaac. The Opera del Duomo Administration judging the works considered best the bas-reliefs by Brunelleschi and Ghiberti. The latter was finally charged with the construction of the door. Ghiberti's elegance and pictorial effect was preferred over Brunelleschi's concentrated, rude conception.
The two interesting reliefs are found at the Museo Nazionale. While keeping the division in 28 parts as in the Southern Door, the artist has impressed in the stories of the New Testament, from the Annunciation to the Pentecost in the 20 upper scenes and to the Evangelists and Doctors of the church in the 8 inferior scenes, a Renaissance-like character through a naturalistic interpretation. The doors-post, decorated with foliage, flowers and animals, are also by Ghiberti. The group of three statues in bronze above the portal representing the *Baptist between the Levite and the Pharisee,* are by G. Francesco Rustici (1506-11).

EASTER DOOR. — It is the one before the facade of the Cathedral. It was called by Michelangelo « the door of Paradise ». This represents Ghiberti's masterpiece which he completed in 27 years of work, from 1425 to 1452.
All the wealth of fantasy, elegance of composition and wisdom of creation is found there. To the projecte cooperated also Michelozzo, Benozzo Gozzoli and Bernardo Cennini. This stupendous work, constantly admired, was recently given the splendour of its ancient gilding. The door is subdivided in 10 parts representing biblical scenes in accordance with themes dictated by Leonardo Bruni, the Chancellor of the Republic at that time. A complete description and illustration of this masterwork is found on pages 24 and 25.

THE BAPTISTERY. - **Lorenzo Ghiberti:** Southern Door.

1 Creation of Adam and Eve; The Original Sin; Expulsion from Paradise.

2 Adam and Eve with Cain and Abel; The Sacrifice to God; The first work: Abel shepherd, Cain at the plough; Cain kills Abel; First example of justice: the Curse of Cain.

3 Story of Noah: His family leaves the ark after the Flood; Noah's thanks-ɩving and the Rainbow; The planting f the Vine and Noah's drunkenness; erided by Ham he is covered by Shem ıd Japhet.

4 Story of Abraham; Sara at the entrance to the tent; Angels appear to Abraham in the valley of Mambre; Journey with Isaac to the Mountain; Angel holds Abraham's arm; The servants await their return.

Story of Jacob and Esau: Esau sells his first birthright; Isaac sends au hunting; Jacob brings the meat his Father and covers his neck with e skin; Isaac mistakes Jacob for au and blesses him; Jacob leaves s Father's house.

6 Story of Joseph: He is put by his brothers in the well; Is sold to the merchants; Is sold by the merchants to Pharaoh; Whose dreams he interprets and foretells the coming famine, counsels provisions; He recognises his brothers and pardons them; Meeting of Joseph and Jacob.

7 Story of Moses: He receives the Tablets of the Law; Joshua waits half way up the mountain; The Israelites wait in fear and trembling at the foot.

8 Story of Joshua: The crossing of the Jordan; The twelve stones taken from the river; The fall of the walls of Jericho; The Israelites take the city.

9 Story of Saul and David: Saul conquers the Philistines; David kills Goliath; And exulting carries the head to the Army.

10 King Solomon solemnly receives the Queen of Sheba.

In the frames of the two doors Ghiberti placed 24 statuettes of Prophets and Sybils alternately with 24 medallions representing artists who were contemporaries of Ghiberti.

LEFT SIDE. Above, the reclining figure represents Spring.

From top to bottom, left: the prophet Amos, the prophet Zacariah, the prophet Daniel, the daughter of Jephtha, Judith.

From top to bottom, right: the prophet Barue, the prophet Elias, the Delphic Sybil, the prophet Isaia, the prophet Haggai.

At the bottom, the reclining figure represents Summer.

RIGHT SIDE. Above, the reclining figure represents Autumm.

From top to bottom left: The Tiberine Sybil, the Persian Sybil, The prophet Elisha, Joshua, the Cuman Sybil.

From top to bottom, right: Judas Maccabeus, Samson, The prophet Jeremiah, Gideon, the prophet Ezechiel.

At the bottom, the reclining figure represents Winter.

The small head almost in the centre of the door, between the Delphic Sybil and the Prophet Isaiah is the self-portrait of Ghiberti. The other between the prophet Elisha and the prophet Joshua, is the portrait of Bartoluccio, step-father of Lorenzo Ghiberti and his master.

Above the door: « The Baptism of Christ » by Andrea Sansovino (1502), the angel is the work of Innocenzo Spinazzi of the 13th century, while the two porphyry columns beside the door, were given to the Florentines by the Pisans in 1117 in gratitude for their generous action while the Pisans were engaged in the war against the Saracens.

THE BAPTISTERY. - **Andrea Sansovino:** « The Baptism of Christ ». The « Angels » is by **Innocenzo Spinazzi.** (Statues on the Architrave of the « Door of Paradise »).

GIOTTO'S BELL-TOWER

This tower, 81,75 meters high, remains to this day (after half a millennium since its construction) a beauty which has no rival of its kind in the whole world. Invited by the Signoria in 1334 Giotto presented the design and, in July of the same year, foundations were laid for the colossal work. However, three years had hardly gone by when Giotto passed away. The work was continued until 1348 by Andrea Pisano and completed by Francesco Talenti in 1359. Let us note, however, that both artists scrupolously followed the designs of the great master with one exception: the terminal spire, which was to add another 30 meters to the height of the tower, was never built.

It is covered with colored marbles and adorned with bas-relief that can be considered unique throughout Italy. The rectangular basement is divided into two ones: in the first are found relief pictures by Andrea Pisano and Luca della Robbia based on Giotto's designs and representing *stories of human labour;* in the second, symbolic figures by Andrea Pisano and Andrea Orcagna. Then follows the portion attributed to Francesco Talenti with the 16 niches in which were found sculptures by Donatello, Nanni di Bartolo and others. These sculptures are now preserved in the Opera del Duomo Museum. The elegance of the architecture of the tower continues as far as the very summit where we see two zones of two-fold windows and then a three-fold final window over which projects the large surbase with the balustrade. From the top one can enjoy a most beautiful view of the city and of the surrounding hills.

The Cathedral (Santa Maria del Fiore). ▶

Loggia del Bigallo. — Before going inside the Cathedral, one may note on the right side, almost opposite the southern door of the Baptistery and cornering with Via dei Calzaioli, the characteristc Loggia del Bigallo of elefant Gothic-florentine architecture. This Loggia is attributed to Alberto Arnoldi, the director of the Opera del Duomo (1352-58). At first the headquarters of the Misericordia, it became later that of another association called « Bigallo ». The purpose of this organization was to expose to the mercy of the citizenry lost or abandoned children. On its facade we can see three tabernacles with *Saint Peter the Martyr*, the *Madonna and Child*, and *Saint Lucia*. These are statues from the school of Nino Pisano (1365). In the underlying lunette we can see the bas-relief of the *Madonna and Child*, by Arnoldo Arnoldi (1361). Two beautiful curved arcades open the Loggia, and a row of two-fold windows are above it. In the interior is particularly interesting the fresco of the *Madonna della Misericordia* with a view of thirteen-century Florence.

THE CATHEDRAL (SANTA MARIA DEL FIORE)

This magnificent building was started by Arnolfo di Cambio in 1296. He was entrusted by the Republic to carry out his work « in such a high and sumptuous magnificence that could be neither better nor more beautiful ly conceived by man's powèr and industry ». It was located in the same place where had once stood the Church of Santa Reparata, the cathedral of Florence opposite the Baptistery of Saint John. Upon Arnolfo's death in 1302, the construction was interrupted and not started again until 1334 under the direction of Giotto who had already supervised the construction of the bell-tower. At his death in 1337 the construction was slowed down and from 1357 until 1364 the Opera del Duomo Administration gave the direction to Lapo Ghini and Francesco Talenti. This time the proportions were bigger than Arnolfo's. At last in 1366 the final version of the project was presented by four architects and the construction proceeded at a faster pace. By 1378 the vault of the central nave had already been completed. From 1380 to 1421 the tribune and the tamburo of the dome were built. As early as 1418, however, a contest was announced for the construction of the dome. It as won by Filippo Brunelleschi who, from 1420 until 1434, accomplished that marvelous architectural monument which is the wonder of the whole world. In 1436 Pope Eugene IV solemnly consacrated the temple and dedicated it Santa Maria del Fiore. The lantern of the cupola was completed in 1461.

THE FACADE. - It was built by the Florentine architect Emilio De Fabris who was inspired by the Gothic-florentine style.

An Aerial view of the Cathedral. ▶

The Median Portal of the Cathedral.

THE CATHEDRAL. — Interior.

He worked from 1871 until 1883 and decorated the facade with statues by contemporary artist. It was then continued by his helper Luigi Del Moro who completed it in 1887. The facade is divided by four pillars with three portals. In the spandrel is the *Eternal Father* by Augusto Passaglia and in the underlying 14 partitions are located the bust of great artists of the past. In the 13 tabernacles above the portals there are statues of the Apostles at the centre of which is the *Madonna and Child* by Tino Sarrocchi. In the tabernacles of the pillars are seen from the left statues of *Bishop Valeriani* who blessed the first stone of the temple; also, a statue of Bishop Tinacci Who blessed the first pillar; one of Pope Eugene IV Who consecrated the temple; one of Saint Antonio Who blessed the facade. The left portal is the work of Passaglia (1897). In the partitions he reproduces the *Presentation of Mary to the Temple*, the *Wedding of the Virgin, Faith, Humility,* and *Prudence.* In the lunette we see a mosaic on a cartoon by Nicolò Barabino reproducing *Enthroned Charity.* The median portal by Passaglia (1903) reproduces the *Conception* and the *Crowning of the Virgin.* In the lunette we see a mosaic by Barabino with *Jesus, the Madonna and the Patrons of the City.* In the fronton we see the *Madonna in Glory* by Passaglia. The right portal is by Giuseppe Cassioli (1889) and reproduces the *Expulsion from Paradise*, the *Assumption*, the *Rest in Egypt*, the *Visitation*, the *Birth of Mary* and the *Annunciation.* In the lunette is found *Worshiped Faith, a* mosaic on cartoon by Barabino.

THE EXTERIOR - The relaying of the building is in marble of three colors: white from Carrara, green from Prato and red from Maremma. It is interesting to note along the right side the Door of the Canonici which was planned and decorated by Giovanni d'Ambrogio and Piero di Giovanni Tedesco, towards the end of the XIV century. On the opposite side, along the left flank, we see the famous door of the Mandorla, from which are visible signs of Renaissance influence. It is so-called because of the shape of the fronton which contains the *Madonna* by Nanni di Banco (1421). The two little statues of the *Prophets* are by the young Donatello (1408). The mosaic in the lunette with the *Annunciation* is by Domenico Ghirlandaio (1491).

THE INTERIOR. - Vast and sober in its decoration, it was appropriate for the very character of the Florentines who wanted the House of the Lord without pleasant ornaments but imposing and austere and very spacious. Shaped like a Latin cross it is divided into three naves by solidly-built yet elegant pillars which suport the huge ogival: a magnificent example of Gothic-florentine architecture. It is about 523 feet long, 140 feet wide at the nave and 297 feet at the cross-vault. - Internal Facade: the colored sash above the three portals were made on cartoons of Lorenzo Ghiberti. The mosaic on the lunette above the median portal representing the *Growning of the Virgin,* is attributed to Gaddo Gaddi (XIV century). At the flanks, under the arcades (of acute arches), there is a fresco of *Angel Musicians* by Santi di Tito (end of the XVI century). Right of the portal, *Antonio d'Orso's Tomb* can be seen; he was a Florentine Bishop of the XIV century, and his tomb was the work of the Senese sculptor Tino di Camaino (XIV century). Way above is a clock the face of which is decorated with heads of prophets by Paolo Uccello (1443). - Right nave: in the first bay is a medallion with *Brunelleschi's Bust,* a work by his pupil Andrea Cavalcanti also called Buggiano (1447). Further ahead can be seen a wooden tabernacle (seemingly of marble) with the *Statue of Isaiah* attributed to Nanni di Banco (1408). In the medallion that follows is *Giotto's Bust* by Benedetto da Maiano (1490) with an epigraph by Poliziano. Of the valuable Gothic holy water stoup at the first pillar (1380) only the base is original, while

The Consecration of the Cathedral, from a Miniature Missal of the XV century kept in the Laurenziana Library.

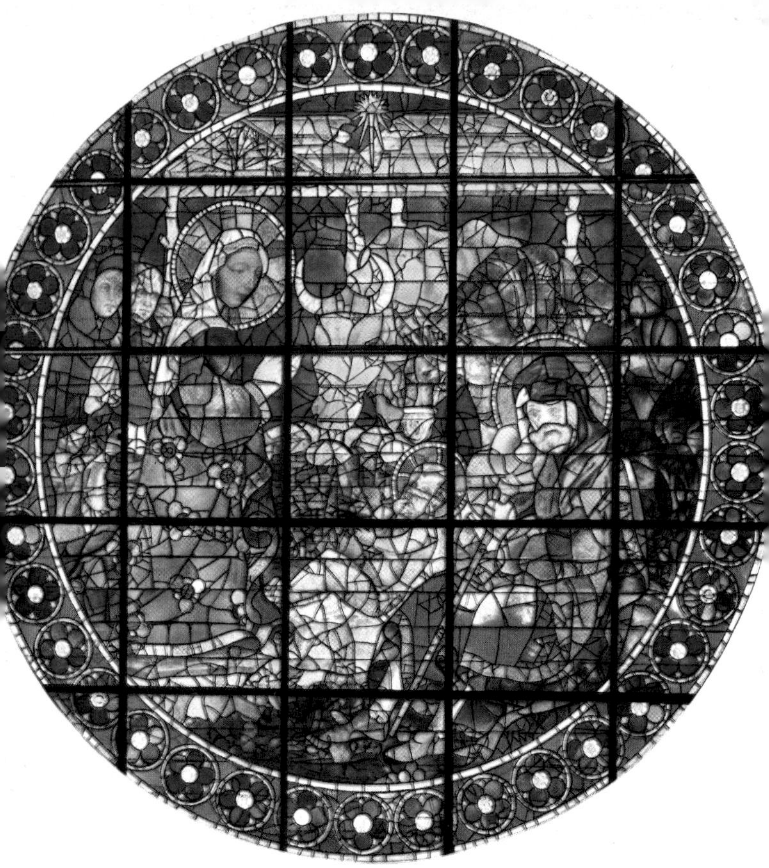

CATHEDRAL. - Stained glass window from cartoons by Paolo Uccello depicting the Nativity.

the Angel and the basin are copies of the original which is preserved in the Opera del Duomo Museum. In the third bay are two false sepulchral monuments painted by Bicci di Lorenzo (XV century). In the medallion of the fourth bay is a marble bust of *Marsilio Ficino* by Andrea Ferrucci (1521). - Let us now go inside the huge octagon dominated by the imposing dome of 297 feet in height without the lantern, and 372 with it; the diameter above the tamburo measures 148,84 feet. The interior of the dome is decorated with the large fresco representing the *Universal Judgement* by Giorgio Vasari and Federico Zuccari (1572-79). The colored sashes of the underlying tamburo were made on cartoons of Ghiberti, Donatello, Paolo Uccello and Andrea del Castagno. In the pillars at the entrance of the tribunes supporting the dome are found niches with eight statues of the Apostles. Of great importance is the statue of *San Giovanni* at the last pillar on the right by Benedetto da Rovezzano; and that of *San Giacomo Maggiore* at the left pillar of the median nave by Iacopo Sansovino. At the center of the octagon is a marble chorus designed by Giuliano di Baccio d'Agnolo and done by Baccio Bandinelli (1555). By the latter are also the bas-reliefs of the marble enclosure that defines the choir but in cooperation with Giovanni Bandini. The *Crucifix* on the High

THE CATHEDRAL. — **Michelangelo:** « Pietà ».

[illegible]ento a N. Marucci, di Andrea del Castagno;

Monumento a Giovanni Acuto, di P. Uccello.

Altar is by Benedetto da Maiano (1497). The three tribunes forming the cross-vault are each divided by five chapels. Between the right and the central tribunes is the entrance to the OLD SACRISTY surmounted by the lunette with varnished terracotta by Luca della Robbia representing the *Ascension* (1450). In the main chapel of the central tribune there is a bronze urn with the relics of San Zanobi. This is a masterpiece by Lorenzo Ghiberti (1432-42) with most beautiful bas-relief representing stories of the Saint. Between the central and left tribune is the entrance to the NEW SACRISTY, or the capel of the Masses, where on A-pril 26, 1478 Lorenzo the Magnificent took refuge. He was fleeing from the Pazzi Conspiracy in which his brother Giuliano found death. In the lunette above the door is the *Resurrection*, a work in terracotta by Luca della Robbia, representing the artist's first experiment in ceramic sculpture. The door in bronze was the work of della Robbia, Michelozzo and Maso di Bartolomeo. It is interesting to notice in the interior of the sacresty the wash-stand by Buggiano (1440) with the Angel head attributed to Mino da Fiesole. The inlaid cupboards are by Giuliano da Maia-no (1465). In the first chapel of the transept is the dramatic marble composition of the *Pietà* by Michelangelo (1550). This work, which constitutes the most important monument existing in the cathedral and which Michelangelo intended to be placed on his tomb, was never completed by the « Titan ». - Left nave: almost at the beginning is the entrance door giving access to the staircase of 463 steps. A very beautiful view can be enjoyed from the summit. At the fourth bay is the famous painting by Domenico di Michelino (1465) representing *Dante and an open book of his Divine Comedy* with Florence at the left, Hell at its right, Purgatory in the background, and Paradise above. Corresponding with the third bay there is an equestrian monument of the *English leader John Hawkwood (Giovanni Acuto),* a fresco transferred on cloth and the work of Paolo Uccello (1436). At the second bay is a monument of *Capitain Niccolò Marucci da Tolentino.* This one also is a fresco transferred on cloth and the work of Andrea del Castagno (1456). We also note a bust of the organist *Antonio Squarcialupi,* by Benedetto da Maiano (1490). In the first bay is a wooden tabernacle with a statue of the *Prophet Joshua* which is believed to represent the humanist Poggio Bracciolini. This work is supposed to be by Ciuffagni and Nanni di Bartolo in cooperation with Donatello.

THE OPERA DEL DUOMO MUSEUM

In the museum are preserved remains of Romanesque architecture: statues and decorations which were once in the cathedral, in the Baptistery and Giotto's Campanile.

In the vestibule we see a *Bust of Brunelleschi,* two works in terracotta by the Della Robbias and marble bas-reliefs by Baccio Bandinelli. At the right one goes inside the first hall where are preserved fragments of the ancient baptismal font of the Baptistery. From here we into the second great hall with statues coming from the facade of the cathedral; of interest are that of *San Giovanni* by Donatello, that of *San Luca* by Nanni di Banco, that of *San Matteo* by Bernardo Ciuffagni. In the background is a statue of *Pope Bonifacio VIII,* from the workshop of Arnolfo It is interesting to note, at the fourth wall, the design reproducing the facade of the cathedral before its demolition in 1588. A door of the fourth wall leads into the the third hall in which are kept missals painted in miniature of many centuries, precious shrines for relics, enamel works as well as valuable works from the cathedral. On the altar of the small chapel, in the background, is found a panel by Bernardo Daddi representing the *Madonna with S. Zanobi and S. Catharine* (1334). Returning into the second hall a staircase leads to the upper floor. In the lobby are reliefs of the life of Jesus reproducing the ornamental works of the first door which was the work of Ghiberti and which he made for the Baptistery. On the door leading into the great hall are two frescoes of heads of Apostles by Bicci di Lorenzo. This great hall is called « delle Cantorie » because here were located the two famous choirs which formerly were above the doors of the two sacresties of the cathedral from which they were removed in 1688. On the wall of the entrance door is the choir of Luca della Robbia (1431-38) with 10 high-reliefs divided by coupled pillars. This is a graciously styled and pleasing work representing boys and girls singing and playing the psalm of David, « Laudate Dominus in sanctis eius ». Opposite this we see the choir by Donatello (1433-38) with winged angels dancing joyopsly and running impetuously on the loggia. In the same hall are the *Moses,* the *Jeremiah,* and the *Abacucco* called « the Zuccone » (big pumpkin): these works by Donatello formerly were in the niches of Giotto's Bell-tower. Also in the same hall, right of the entrance, is the *Sacrifice of Isac* by Donatello and

THE CATHEDRAL. — **Domenico di Michelino**: « Dante explaining his Divine Comedy ».

Detail of the Choir Gallery, by **Donatello.**

Detail of the Choir Gallery, by **Luca della Robbia.**

MEDICI-RICCARDI PALACE. - The Chapel.

Nanni di Bartolo, and along the walls are sculptures of sibyls and prophets by Andrea Pisano. From the right corner of the hall one enters the fifth hall where are preserved various and valuable pictorial works as well as sculptures. For example, the *Madonna and Saints* by Bernardo Daddi (1334); *Martyrdom of Saint Sebastian* and stories of His life, a triptych by Giovanni del Biondo (XIV cent.); inlaid woodwork with *San Zanobi and two Saints*, by Giuliano da Maiano; a *Woman with Cornucopia* by Tino di Camaino. Interesting also are the 27 embroidered works, 18 by the entrance wall and 9 by the front wall, with stories of the life of Saint John made from the of Antonio del Pollaiuolo (1466-80). At the back wall is the famous and very valuable reredos in silver and enamel with stories of Saint John the Baptist, a masterpiece cartoons carried out by the best Florentine artists during 114 years of work, from the XIV to the XV centuries: Andrea del Verrocchio sculptured the beheading, Antonio del Pollaiolo sculptured the birth of the Baptist, Bernardo Cennini sculptured the visitation of Saint Elizabeth. The central statue of the Baptist in the front part is the work of Michelozzo and the cross on the reredos was the work of Betto Betti, Milano Dei and Antonio del Pollaiolo. Returning into the Cantorie one enters the last hall where are exposed the various projects and models of the dome and of the lantern as well as the model for the decoration of the tamburo. In the glass case is the funeral mask of Filippo Brunelleschi.

Coming out of the museum, we suggest to the tourist to go towards the right (alongside the left side of the cathedral) and enter via Martelli.

Via de' Martelli. — It is the meeting place of the Florentines and one of the most lively streets in the city with many shops and well-supplied bookshops. On the left we come across the MARTELLI PALACE (where the Galilei Lyceum is at present), and further ahead, is the CHRCH OF SAN GIOVANNINO the facade of which is by Ammannati (XVI cent.) and in the interior are frescoes and cloths by artists of the XVI-XVII century. At the opposite corner, where the street becomes via Cavour, we see the Medici-Riccardi Palace.

THE MEDICI-RICCARDI PALACE

It is a superb building having the character of pure Renaissance. Cosimo the Elder commissioned Michelozzo Michelozzi (1444-60) who was one of Brunelleschi's pupils and who reached here his architectural masterpiece. In years to follow this superb building was to become the residence of Lorenzo il Magnifico. This majestic and elegant palace has three floors with beautiful, arched windows and a rich, harmonious cornice. The windows of the ground floor were added in the XVI century and those near the corner were designed by Michelangelo. In 1659 the palace was bought by the Riccardi family who enlarged it on the side of via Ginori and added 7 more windows to the original 10. The palace passed then into the hands of the Tuscan government (1814) and ultimately into the hands of the Italian government. As of now it is the headquarters of the Prefettura.

From the imposing portal one enters the court-yard in which is a very beautiful columned patio and an open gallery with Ionic columns at the second boor. This gallery was used as a model by many XV ventury palaces. On the architrave above the arches the medallions are attributed to Bertoldo, while the blask leads are by Maso di Bartolomeo (1452). From the court-yard, through a door at the left, one can enter the MEDICI MUSEUM where are kept objects of artistic value, documents and old curiosities that testify the istory and glories of the Medici family. Of significance is a *Madonna and Child* by Filippo Lippi (1450); also a series of little Medici portraits, among which those of the sons of Cosimo I: all by Bronzino the court portrait-painter; also a funeral mask of Lorenzo de' Medici. - Coming back into the court-yard through a staircase we go into the CHAPEL designed by Michelozzo who also designed the attic, the stall and the floor. The interior is a real wonder of colors, of customs and portraits of the Magi to *Bethlehem*. The artist has represented personalities of the period and, above all, of the Medici family: the youngest of the Magi represents Lorenzo the Magnificent as a young man. On the altar, is a *Madonna in prayer and Child*, a free copy by Neri di Bicci from an original by Filippo Lippi. Once we have returned to the court-yard, we take the other stairs under the porch and go up to the baroque gallery, built from 1670 to 1688 the volt of which was painted by Luca Giordano (1683) with scenes of the Apotheosis of the Medici Dynasty, a work of great decorative value.

Once we have left the palace, turning to the right along the left flank of the building, is the short via dei Gori which leads into piazza San Lorenzo.

MEDICI-RICCARDI PALACE. - **Benozzo Gozzoli:** « Voyage of the Three Kings ». (Detail)

MEDICI-RICCARDI PALACE. — **Benozzo Gozzoli:** « Voyage of the Three Kings ». (Detail).

Piazza San Lorenzo. — This picturesque and lively square was in former times the Market Place. It is dominated by the huge Church of Saint Lawrence behind which rises the dome of the Principal Chapel. At the beginning we note the monument to *Giovanni delle Bande Nere*, the work of Baccio Bandinelli (1540) who also made the valuable reliefs around the base.

THE CHURCH OF SAN LORENZO

Of very ancient origin, it was erected on the same spot where once had stood a church consecrated in 393 by Saint Ambrose, the Bishop of Milan. Built in Romanesque style around the year 1000, it was rebuilt as we now see it by Filippo Brunelleschi (1421-46) after sponsorship of Giovanni Bicci de' Medici. The work was continued by the pupil Antonio Manetti who completed it in 1460. Always after the Medici sponsorship Michelangelo designed the internal facade, the new sacresty and the library and made the project for the external facade which has remained unfinished.

THE INTERIOR. - It is composed of three naves divided by Corynthian columns of agile and elegant appearance with the typically Brunelleschian decoration of stone over white plaster. The whole is serenity and harmony at their highest. The balcony high in the internal facade is the work of Michelangelo. The two pulpits in the two last spans of the central nave, on the right and on the left, are the last work of Donatello.
Since he died in 1466, he was unable to bring them to completion. They were later finished by his pupils Bertoldo and Bellano. Special attention deserve the panel of the *Cricifiction* and the *Deposition from the Cross* (of the left pulpit) because of their intense dramatic appeal. In the second chapel of the right nave is a painting of the *Wedding of the Virgin* by Rosso Fiorentino; at the end of the nave is a very beautiful tabernacle in marble, the work of Desiderio da Settignano (XV century). The big fresco at the extremity of the left nave, representing the *Martyrdom of Saint Lawrence*, is the work of Bronzino (1569). At the bottom of the steps of the high altar three gratings in bronze indicate the spot in which is buried Cosimo the Elder, called Pater Patriae. From the corner of the left arm of the transept one has access into the OLD SACRESTY which was designed by Brunelleschi who left it the mark of his style which is here of exquisite balance and harmonic rythm.. It is a square plan with a hemispheric dome. The medallions of the pendentives of the dome in coloured stucco with *stories of Saint John the Baptist* are by Donatello. By the same artist are also: the four *Evangelists* in the lunettes; the frieze of *Cherubs;* the two portals in bronze at the sides of the high altar in the panels of which are figures of the *Apostles* and of the *Doctors of the Church;* the very beautiful *bust of Saint Lawrence* in terracotta above the bench. In the sarcophagus at the centre, sculptured by Andrea Cavalcanti called Buggiano, are buried Giovanni dei Bicci de' Medici, the father of Cosimo the

Elder, and his wife Piccarda. The sarcophagus at the left under the arch, in porphyry and bronze, a masterpiece of Verrocchio (1472), contains the corpses of Giovanni and Piero de' Medici, the sons of Cosimo the Elder.
Once we have returned into the church we note, on the right, the MARTELLI CHAPEL of the XIV century with a wonderful *Annunciation* on the altar by Filippo Lippi. At the wall is the *tomb of Donatello* by Romanelli (1896). From the door cornering with the chapel one has access into the great cloister and the Laurenziana Library.

The Laurenziana Library. — One may enter it through entrance No. 9 of Piazza San Lorenzo, at the left of the church, by crossing the very beautiful cloister by Brunelleschi of 1457. Through a staircase one arrives at the library founded by Cosimo the Elder and enlarged by Lorenzo. Built, as far as architecture an decoration are concerned, on designs by Michelangelo, he built the vestibule beginning it in 1524 and completed later by Vasari and other architects. The huge hall, over 163 feet long, has 15 glass windows designed by Giovanni da Udine. The wooden attic, the benches and the lecterns were designed by Michelangelo. The great library is one of the most famous in the world and contains a most precious, splendid collection of codes, manuscripts and missals in miniature from the VI to the XV century, besides the prayer book of Lorenzo the Magnificent and a very important collection of autographs, from that of Petrarch to that of Napoleon, all of incalculable value.

From the square and turning left always along the exterior of the church, we arrive at the Madonna degli Aldobrandini Square where is found the entrance to the Medici Chapels.

MEDICI CHAPELS

The construction of this marvelous building was started in 1604 by Matteo Nigetti, after a designs by Prince Giovanni de' Medici, the natural brother of Grand Duke Cosimo I, who wanted here the sepulchre of the Medici family, a place worthy of their power and wealth. It was in fact called the chapel of the Princes.

One enters a vast crypt from which one goes up to the Baroque chapel of the Princes with the walls entirely covered with precious marbles, with hard stones finely worked and with gilt bronze works. The frescoes of the dome, with *scenes form the Old and New Testament*, are by Piero Benvenuti (1829). In the inferior portion of the walls are represented the 16 coats-of-arms of the Grand-duchy, in marble mosaic and precious stones. The six sarcophagi in porphyry belong to the Medici Grand-dukes from Cosimo I to Cosimo III. The statues in bronze are by Pietro Tacca (XVII century). Behind the very rich altar in hard stones two little chapels preserve ancient reliquaries and golden objects of very great value. Returning towards the entrance wall, from the left one has access into the NEW SACRESTY, so called in order to distinguish it from the old in the church of Saint Lawrence, of which it preserves the same plan, but differs from it with its austere appearance of a sepulchral chapel. The work of Michelangelo, it was put there by Vasari in 1557. The great Miche-

MEDICI CHAPELS. — The Tombs of the Princes.

langelo wanted to give, in the architectural as well as in the sculptural parts, a solemn and imposing appearance. Here are found the three famous tombs, of which only two were completed. The one by the wall left of the entrance is the *tomb of Lawrence the Duke of Urbino,* the nephew of Lawrence the Magnificent, here represented in a thoughtful mood, with the two figures lying on the sarcophagus symbolizing *Dawn* and *Dusk.* The other in the front is the *tomb of Giuliano the duke of Nemours,* the son of Lorenzo il Magnifico, who is shown seated with

MEDICI CHAPELS. — **Pietro Benvenuti:** Frescoes in the Cupola.

MEDICI CHAPELS. - The New Sacristy.

his armour and his stick of authority, a symbol of action; at his feet are two symbolic figures of *Day* and *Night*. At the right wall is the monument which was to be destined to Lawrence the Magnificent and his brother Giuliano, here buried, ha remained unfinished. Michelangelo sculptured the Madonna and Child which we can admire in the features of a very young figure of a calm and serene nobility. The figure of Saints Cosma and Damiano have been the work of Michelangelo's pupils: Montorsoli and Raffaello da Montelupo.

MEDICI CHAPELS. - The richly decorated altar in semi-precious stones.

MEDICI CHAPELS. - **Michelangelo:** Tomb of Giuliano, Duke of Nemours.

MEDICI CHAPELS. - **Michelangelo:** Tomb of Lorenzo, Duke of Urbino.

SECOND ITINERARY

PIAZZA DEL DUOMO - VIA DEI CALZAIUOLI - CHURCH OF ORSANMICHELE - PIAZZA DELLA SIGNORIA (LOGGIA DELLA SIGNORIA; PALAZZO VECCHIO) - UFFIZI SQUARE (UFFIZI GALLERY).

Via dei Calzaiuoli. — It is one of the main arteries of the city, flanked by elegant shops, which joins the Cathedral Square with the Signoria Square. At the beginning, on the right, an inscription indicates the place where were the « workshops » (botteghe) of Donatello and Michelozzo. Past Via Tosinghi, on the left, we see the crossroad of Via del Corso (the ancient road in which took place the races of the Berbers), and on the right is Via degli Speziali which leads to the modern Republic Square. Further on, always proceeding towards Signoria Square, we find, on the right, a square, gothic building looking almost like a dungeon with the characteristics of civile construction, but, in faet, a religious building: it is the Church of Orsanmichele.

THE CHURCH OF ORSANMICHELE

It was built by Arnolfo di Cambio in 1290 at which time the ancient church of Saint Michael the Archangel was demolished. It was then flanked by an orchard (from which derives Saint Michael in the Orchard), and was used as the Wheat Market. When a fire destroyed the contsruction by Arnolfo, in the XIV century it was rebuilt. To this reconstruction took part those architects of that period who were also in charge of other city projects; among these artists are to be mentioned Francesco Talenti, Neri di Fioravante, Benci di Cione and Simone di Francesco Talenti. These citizens raised the loggia of one floor in order to have a wheat deposit able to meet all the needs of the citizens in case of an emergency. The construction, by order of the Florentine Republic, was begun in 1337 and completed in 1404. Even as early as the construction in 1349, it was decided to transform the loggia into an oratory. Thus, in 1380 Simone di Francesco Talenti was given the task to cover up the arcades. He carried out

The exterior of the Church of Orsanmichele (detail).

his duty magnificently by closing them with very beautiful portals ornamented with drillings as light as laces; while in the tabernacles of the pillars were located statues of the Saint protectors of the Major Arts. These statues constitute an eloquent documentary of the development of Florentine sculpture from the XIV to the XVI centuries.

Beginning on the left on the side of Via de' Calzaiuoli, we see: 1) a Tabernacle of the Art of Calimala, with *Saint John the Baptist,* by Lorenzo Ghiberti (1414-16); 2) a Tabernacle of the Tribunal of Merchandise, by Donatello and Michelozzo with *Christ and Saint Thomas,* a bronze by Andrea del Verrocchio (1464-83); 3) a Tabernacle of the Art of the Judges and Notaries, with *Saint Luke,* by Giambologna (1601). Continuing on the side of Via Orsanmichele: 1) a Tabernacle of the Art of the Butchers, with *Saint Peter,* by Donatello (1408); 2) a Tabernacle of Shoemakers, with *Saint Philip,* by Nanni di Banco (1405-10); 3) a Tabernacle of Constructors and Sculptors, with four *Crowned Saints,* by Nanni di Banco (1408); 4) a Tabernacle of Gunsmiths, with *Saint George,* by Donatello (1416). a copy of the original which is found at the National Museum.

Continuing along Via dell'Arte della Lana we see: 1) a Tabernacle of Cambio's Art, with *Saint Matthew,* by Lorenzo Ghiberti (1420); a Tabernacle of the Art of Wool, with *Saint Stephen,* by Lorenzo Ghiberti (1428); 3) a Tabernacle of the Art of the Farriers, with *Saint Eligio,* by Nanni di Banco (1415). Between the two left tabernacles is the main entrance into the church with sculpture by Nicholas Lamberti. On the side of Via dei Lamberti are

CHURCH OF ORSANMICHELE. - **Andrea del Verrocchio:** « Christ and Saint Thomas » (Tabernacle of the Tribunal of Merchandise, by **Donatello** and **Michelozzo**).

A suggestive view of Piazza della Signoria.

CHURCH OF ORSANMICHELE. — **Andrea Orcagna:** The Tabernacle.

found: 1) a Tabernacle of the Art of Flax Workers, with *Saint Mark*, by Donatello (1411-13); 2) a Tabernacles of the Art of Fur Dealers, with *San Iacopo* and a bas-relief, attributed to Ciuffagni; 3) a Tabernacle of Physician and Druggists, with a *Madonna and Child*, also called Madonna of the Rose, attributed to Simone Talenti; 4) a Tabernacle of the Art of Silk, with *Saint John the Evangelist*, by Baccio da Montelupo (1515). The medallions in terracotta are by Luca della Robbia; that of the Art of the Butchers is modern and from the Ginori factory.
We can reach the interior through a small door which opens on the side of Via de' Calzaiuoli, as well as through the main portal on the side of Via dell'Arte della Lana.

THE INTERIOR. It is a simple rectangular room in two naves on pillars which support the vaults with frescoes of the fourteenth and fifteenth centuries dedicated to Saints protectors of the Minor Arts. At the right nave is a wonderful TABERNACLE by Andrea di Cione, called Orcagna (1349-59) which stands out with its rich statuettes, arabesques, angels and saint as well as very valuable bas-relief representing stories of the Virgin. It is a true masterpiece of the flowery Gothic style of which the influence was felt in Florence towards the middle of the XIV century. The bas-reliefs around the base depict: the *Birth of the Virgin*; *Presentation at the Temple;* the *Wedding; Annunciation; Adoration of the Magi; Presentation of Jesus at the Temple*; *Announcement to Mary of Her Near End.* Above are little statues of *Angels, Prophets, Sibyls, Virtues,* and *Apostles,* and at the summit of the little dome, is the *Redeemer.* Among the bas-reliefs the most valuable is that of the *Death of the Virgin,* and *Her Assumption,* on the back of the altar; the beardless figure covered by a hood, is the self-portrait of Orcagna. On the altar we see the *Madonna delle Grazie* (Madonna of the Miracles), a work by Bernardo Daddi (1352).

On the left altar is a marble group depicting the *Virgin and Saint Ann,* a work by Francesco da Sangallo (1526).

Coming out of the church from the main portal one sees, on the opposite side, the PALACE OF THE ARTE DELLA LANA, joined with the church by a fly-over bridge. Built in 1300, it was the headquarters of one of the richest corporations in the city; since 1905 when it was restaured, it is the headquarters of the Dante Society. In the interior are found remains of fifteenth-century frescoes. On the corner of the palace is a Gothic tabernacle called Santa Maria della Tromba, with a painting representing the *Virgin with Angels and Saints,* and the *Crowning of the Virgin,* by Iacopo Landini called Casentino (XIV century); originally the tabernacle was in the square of the Old Market, and was transported here when the old centre of the city was demolished.

Returning to Via de' Calzaiuoli, opposite the building of Orsanmichele, is located the small CHURCH OF SAN CARLO DEI LOMBARDI which was begun in 1349 by Neri di Fioravante and Benci di Cione and ended in 1334 by Simone Talenti. In the interior is a valuable painting representing *Christ being placed in the Sepulchre,* by Niccolò Gerini. The latter is a painting of intense dramatic style (XIV century).

PIAZZA DELLA SIGNORIA

Of incomparable beauty and solemnity, it is dominated by the majestic Palazzo Vecchio, by the Loggia of Signoria, by the ancient constructions that surround it, by the big fountain and by numerous monuments. The whole creates an unforgettable vision of grandeur and power. It was here, as a matter of fact, that for many centuries took place great political and historical events as well as the development of the life of Florence in its internal struggles, in its declaration of power and in its messages of civilization to the world.

Before going on to visit the imposing Old Palace and the surrounding statues, it would be wise to look first at the monuments and palace of the square. Left of the facade of the palace, rises the imposing *Fountain* by Bartolommeo Ammannati (1563-75), at

PIAZZA DELLA SIGNORIA. — **Bartolomeo Ammannati:** Neptune

the centre of which is the awkward, gigantic statue of Neptune, called by the Florentines « Biancone » (big, white figure) on account of its candid mass. This work was not too much appreciated by the Florentines who exclaimed, « Oh. Ammannato, Ammannato, che bel marmo hai rovinato). Very beautiful indeed are the bronze statues decorating the basin of the fountain and representing naiads and satyrs by the same Ammannati and others among whom Giambologna. A few yards away from the fountain, towards the centre of the square, is a disc in porphyry with an epigraph which reminds us of the spot on which Father Girolamo Savonarola, the courageous and fighting reformer of the customs of the period, was hanged and burned on the 23 of May 2498 together with His followers Father Dominic Buonvicini from Pisa and Father Silvester Maruffi.
Left of the fountain rises the equestrian statue of *Cosimo I de' Medici*, a work by Giambologna (1594); the three bas-reliefs at the base represent the *Tuscan Senate conferring the Title of Grand-duke to Cosimo I*, 1537; *Pius V gives Cosimo the Granducal insignia*, 1569; the *Entrance of Cosimo into Siena*, 1557. In the bakground, where the square forms an indentation, at N° 10 rises the fourteenth century PALACE OF THE TRIBUNAL OF MERCHANDISE; on the left, N° 7, is the UGUCCIONI PALACE with sixteenth century characteristics and built after a design by Mariotto di Zanobi. Opposite the Old Palace, is the Palace of Insurances by the architect Landi (1871) of a false Medieval-florentine style.

PIAZZA DELLA SIGNORIA. — **Palazzo della Signoria (or Palazzo Vecchio).** ▶

LOGGIA DELLA SIGNORIA. — **Giambologna:**
« Rape of the Sabine Women ».

Loggia della Signoria.

LOGGIA OF THE SIGNORIA

Right of the Old Palace rise the elegant, airy three arcades of the Loggia of the Signoria; a rare example of late Gothic style with pre-Renaissance characteristics. It was also called the LANZI LOGGIA because in the XVI century the Lanzichenecchis were guarding the place after orders of Cosimo I and, it was also called the LOGGIA OF ORCAGNA after a design supposed to be by the artist Orcagna. The construction was by the same architects of the Cathedral; namely, Benci di Cione, Simone Talenti and others from 1376 to 1381. It was erected for the election and proclamation of the Priori and of the Gonfaloniere and for other ceremonies of the Signoria. The sculpture masterpieces under the loggia, belonging to different periods, form a wonderful open-air museum.

At the sides of the staircase that leads into the loggia are found two marble lions. The one at the right is a sculpture of the classical era, while the one on the left is a copy of the Roman sculptor Flaminio Vacca (1600).
Under the loggia are gathered ancient Roman sculptures and works by sculptors of the 16th century in Florence. On the parapet of the left arch is the famous *Perseus*, a bronze masterwork by Benvenuto Cellini (1533). Perseus is represented holding high a cut-off head with an expression of conscious strength and is looking with an attitude of profound release at the corpse of Meduso from whose neck flows a great deal of blood. The very fine base presents four niches in which are conveniently placed small statues in bronze representing Mercury, Minerva, Zeus and Danae;

LOGGIA DELLA SIGNORIA. - On the left, « Hercules and the Centaur Nessus » by **Giambologna**; on the right, « Menelaus holding the body of Patroclus » a restored copy from a Greek original of the IV century B. C.

the latter two being Perseus' parents. Further below, we see the bas-relief representing *Perseus in the process of liberating Andromeda*: It is a copy of the original which is preserved at the National Museum. On the parapet of the right arch is the *Rape of the Sabines*, a famous marble group by Giambologna (1583) - this is considered his masterpiece. The bas-relief on the pedestal, also by Giambologna, represents an episode of the epic, historical, Roman event of the rape of the Sabines. Beneath the loggia, on the right, is *Hercules and the Centaur Nessus*, a work of Giambologna (1599); at the centre, is *Menelaus holding the body of Patroclus*, a restored copy from a Greek original of the IV century B.C.; on the left is the *Rape of Polyxena*, a work by the sculptor Pio Fedi (1866). At the back wall are six statues of female, Roman figures of the imperial period representing matrons, vestals and priestesses with the exception of the third on the left representing the figure of Tusnelda or conquered Germany in an expression of profound sorrow.

LOGGIA DELLA SIGNORIA. - **Benvenuto Cellini**: « The Perseus ».

Entrance into the Signoria Palace. (At the left, a copy of the « David » by Michelangelo; at the right, « Hercules and Cacus » by Baccio Bandinelli; above the door, a cuspidated frieze with monogramme of Christ by San Nernardino »).

PALAZZO VECCHIO (OLD PALACE, OR SIGNORIA PALACE)

It is the main architectural monument in Florence and one of the most significant public medieval palaces in Italy. It rises majestically and severely with a tower (307 feet high) which dashes forth directly from the facade with boldness of construction, thus giving a special appearence of elegance to the severe building. It was built, according to tradition, by the genius Arnolfo di Cambio from 1298 to 1314. He supposedly used as a model the castle of the Counts Guidi by Poppi. The original construction is a big parallelepiped in rough ashlar with very beautiful Gothic mullioned windows at the two floors and crowned by a large embattled gallery.
The tower, called Arnolfo's ,is located on the Forabaschi; the terminal pole supports the lilly and the lion, emblems of Florence. The building has undergone additions through the years. To be noted are those in 1343 on the side of Via della Ninna; from 1495 to 1511, on Via dei Gondi and finally, by orders of Cosimo I, the building received additions on its eastern side by Buontalenti (1593), and was completely restored by Vasari without any alterations to the severe exterior appearance.

High in the facade, between the spaces of the little arches supporting the gallery, are painted the emblems of the Republic. On the entrance door is a cuspidated frieze with two lions (1528) at the centre of which is the monogram of Christ by San Bernardino with the inscription, « Rex Regum et Dominus Dominatium » the King of Kings and the Lord of Lords). This sign, placed here in 1851, commemorates the last years of liberty of the republic when the Florentines elected Christ as their King (1529). In the palace, the ancient abode of the Signoria, lived the Duke of Athens (1342-43) and, later Cosimo I de' Medici, from 1540 to 1550 when he transferred with his family and followers to the Pitti Palace. In the periods 1848-49 and 1859-60 it was the headquarters of the provisional governments and in 1865-71 of the Chamber of Deputies of the Kingdom of Italy. Since 1872 the palace is the headquarters of City Hall.

On the level ground of the staircase, opposite the palace, and from which in ancient times orators harangued the people and for this reason it was called « Arringhiera », are located important sculptures. From the left: the *Marzocco*, a symbolic lion of the Florentine Republic which is holding, sitting down, the coat-of-arms with the lilly of Florence, a copy in stone of the original by Donatello (1438) which is found at the National Museum; further on the right on a column, is Giuditta and Oloferne, a bronze by Donatello (1460) considered the symbol of liberty and located here to remind of the expulsion of the Duke of Athens out of Florence; it is interesting to note the picturesque relief at the base. Near the entrance door of the palace, is a copy of *David*, by Michelangelo the original of which was here from 1503 to 1873 and then brought to the Academy Gallery; as a contrast we see the marble group representing *Hercules and Cacus*, by Baccio Bandinelli (1533). At the sides of the portal are two boundaries: the one on the left, by Vincenzo de' Rossi and the one on the right by Bandinelli: they were used to hold the chain that closed the entrance.

THE INTERIOR. Past the entrance door, we note in all its splendour the harmonious and evocative beauty of the arcaded courtyard renewed in Renaissance style by Michelozzo, in 1453. The decoration of the columns (reccently brought back to their original and vivacious heightening) and the frescos of the walls representing the possessions of Austria, were made in 1565 in occasion of the wedding of Francesco de' Medici with Giovanna d'Austria. At the centre of the courtyard is located the fountain in porphyry designed by Giorgio Vasari and made by Battista del Tadda (1557), surmounted by the very gracious, winged genietto (little genius) with the fish. The original copy was by Verrocchio (1476) and it has been recently removed for conservation reasons and actually exposed in the hall of the Cancelleria at the second floor of the palace. In the niche under the portico, is a marble group with *Sanpson and the Philistine*, by Pierino da Vinci. In the corner at the left is the door leading into the Weapons Room, one of the few places left from the fourteenth century construction. Through an entrance hall, almost opposite the entrance door, on can observe the second courtyard with the powerful pillars (built by Cronaca) which support the upper Hall of the Five Hundreds which is reached through one of the two staircases by Vasari placed at the beginning of the entrance hall.

FIRST FLOOR. The HALLL OF THE FIVE HUNDREDS (173 feet long, 71 wide, and 58 high), was built by Simone del Pollaiolo called Cronaca (1495) at the time of the Republic of Savonarola and designed at the meeting of the Great Assembly of the People formed by 500 citizens, after the expulsion of the Medicis in 1494. When the Medicis were restored in 1512, Cosimo I entrusted Baccio d'Agnolo and Baccio Bandinelli with the task of transforming completely the hall so that it could be used for receptions and public assemblies. Later Giorgio Vasari, a painter, an architect and a historian, made the hall larger and put frescoes on the huge walls (1560-72). In the preceding period (1503) Michelangelo and Leonardo da Vinci were entrusted by Gonfaloniere Pier Soderini to decorate the hall with episodes of the history of Florence. But the work of the two great maestros ended at its birth: Leonardo limited himself to designing the battle of Anghiari and Michelangelo an episode of the Pisan war; the cartoons of such designs were later lost or destroyed. The attic of the hall ,divided into 39 partitions, has as many panels painted by Vasari and helpers depicting the history of Florence and of the Medicis ,with the triumph of Cosimo I at the centre. The big frescoes of the walls were the work of Vasari and represent the triumphs of Cosimo I and the episodes of the wars of the decorations beginning from the entrance wall represent: above, *Cosimo I founds the order of the Knights of Saint*

PALAZZO VECCHIO. - **Michelozzo**: Courtyard.

PALAZZO VECCHIO. — Hall of the Five Hundreds.

Stephen, by Passignano; further below in the three large partitions, are 1) *The Florentines defeat the Pisans at Torre San Vincenza;* 2) the *Emperor Maximilian tries to capture leghorn;* 3) *The Florentines attacking Pisa.* At the right extremity above is *Bonifacius VIII receiving Florentine Ambassadors*, by Ligozzi; below, is a statue by *Cosimo I* by Bandinelli. The arras beneath the frescoes are of the Medici School and get inspiration from the stories of Saint John the Baptist, from the frescoes of Andrea del Sarto in the cloister of Via Cavour. Along the wall; are six statues representing the *Fatigues of Hercules* by Vincenzo de' Rossi.

The door at the extremity of the wall, generally closed, leads into the SHELTER decorated by Lorenzo Sabatini and into the HALL OF THE OTTO DI PRATICA, with the very beautiful wooden attic by Benedetto da Maiano and Marco del Tasso, and the walls decorated with arrases of the Gobelins factory (XVIII century). From the back of the shelter, one goes into the HALL OF THE TWO HUNDERTS, so called because here used to gather, during the days of of the Republic, the council of 200 citizens who made important decisions. The construction of the hall is due to Benedetto and Giuliano da Maiano (1472-77); the latter is the author of the very beautiful attic decorated with engraved lillies. At the walls are very beautiful arrases of Florentine manufacture, representing stories of Joseph. These places are actually occupied by the Town Council.

PALAZZO DELLA SIGNORIA. - **Michelangelo:** Victory.

Continuing the visit at the hall of the Five Hundreds, we pass to the wall left of the entrance which has the three big arcaded windows and the floor raised on which used to take seat the Grand-duke during public audiences: this part of the hall was for a good reason called the AUDIENCE. In the three niches, from the left, is a statue by *Giovanni delle Bande Nere*, by Bandinelli; at the centre, is *Leo X*, by Bandinelli and Vincenzo de' Rossi; at the right, is *Alessandro de' Medici*, by Bandinelli. Right wall, from the left: in the niche, is *Pope Clement VII crowning Charles V*, a marble group by Bandinelli and Giovanni Caccini; further on the right, is a statue by Francesco I, by Caccini; above, is Cosimo receiving the insignia from Pius V, painted on blackboard by Cigoli. Then follow three big frescoes by Vasari which depict: 1) the *Capture of Siena*, 2) the *Capture of Porto Ercole;* 3) the *Victory of Marciano*. High, on the right, *Cosimo proclaimed Duke by the Florentine Senate*, by Cigoli. At the back wall at the right, in the central niche, is a marble group by Michelangelo (1525) depicting the *Victory of the Mind over Brutal Strength*, destined to the tomb of Giulius II and here located in 1921 to commemorate the Italian victory of Vittorio Veneto in 1918. In the lateral niches are four ancient, restored statues representing *Leda, Mercury, Apollo and Bacchus*.
From the small glass door at the left extremity of the entrance wall, one enters the LITTLE STUDIO OF FRANCESCO I. It is a small and gracious room all adorned with paintings, frescoes, and little bronze statues and with stucco decorations and incisions, which was built by Giorgio Vasari (1570-72) for the relaxation of the prince who was both a scholar and a lover of beauty. The panels on the ceiling are by Francesco Morandini, called Poppi. In the lunettes the portraits of *Cosimo I* and *Eleonor of Toledo* are by Bronzino. The doors of the cupboards have paintings of several « mannerists » of the sixteenth century, among whom are Bronzino and Allori, that depict mythological and historical episodes. In the eight niches, high in the walls, are located gracious bronze statuettes depicting mythological divinities. It is interesting to note that of *Apollo* by Giambologna, the last of the right wall and that of *Venus* by Ammannati, the last of the opposite wall. From the left wall, through a small door, one can enter the TESORETTO room, the secret writing room of Cosimo I, another creation by Vasari which is also richly decorated by him and his helpers. Here the Grand-duke used to jelously guard the precious objects of his rich collection.
Returning into the Hall of the Five-hundreds, through the glass door on the opposite wall, one enters the Quarters of Leo X (not always visible as it is presently occupied by the offices of the Mayor). The halls, decorated and frescoed by Vasari and helpers with episodes of the life of the Medicis, take the name of personages of the Medici family: ROOM OF LEO X which is adjoined with a little chapel in which is found an old copy of the *Madonna dell'Impannata*, by Raphael; room of CLEMENT VII, with the fresco of Florence besieged in 1529; room of GIOVANNI DELLE BANDE NERE; ROOM OF COSIMO THE ELDER; ROOM OF LAWRENCE THE MAGNIFICENT, ROOM OF COSIMO I.

SECOND FLOOR. — From the hall of Leo X, by going up a steep staircase, we arrive at the second floor (one can also make use of the elevator, but this would necessitate returning to the Hall of the Five Hundreds, and ringing the bell in the shelter at the left of the statue of Victory). On the left of the last floor one enters the QUARTERS OF THE ELEMENTS built by Bernardo del Tasso (1550) and so called because of the frescoes by Vasari and Christopher Gherardi called the Doceno. The elements here represented are *fire, water, land, air* and scenes exalting glories of the Medicis. From the hall of the Elementes we pass into the

PALAZZO VECCHIO. - Hall of Lillies: a detail of a fresco of feigned architecture by **Domenico Ghirlandaio** and helpers.

INGENIVS
DIACONVS

BALCONY OF SATURN, so called on account of the allegory in the ceiling with *Saturn devouring his children.* From here one can enjoy a panoramic view of the city, of the hills of Settignano, of the Piazzale Michelangelo and of the Belvedere Fort. From the left one enters the ROOM OF HERCULES, with the ceiling frescoed by Gherardi with the *Fatigues of Hercules* and at the wall a Florentine arras of the XVI century with *Hercules killing the Centaur* made on a cartoon by Stradano. From THE ROOM OF ZEUS, with the fresco of the *Childhood of Zeus* in the ceiling, we reenter the hall of the elements. From here, through a door at the right, we enter the *Room of Berecinzia* and the *Four Seasons* in the ceiling; at the walls are Florentine arrases with allegorical figures. Then follows the ROOM OF CERERE, with the fresco depicting *Cerere in search of Proserpine,* by Gherardi; at the walls are seen arrases made on cartoons by Stradano which represent the chase after the hedgehog and the bagder. Through a door in the back one enters the WRITING ROOM or hall of Galliope, on account of Vasari's fresco on the ceiling. In this hall Cosimo I spent his time putting in order his collection of precious objects of jewelry, miniatures and bronzes which are now found in the Pitti palace.

Coming out of the Quarters of the Elements, we cross the gallery from which one has a beautiful view from above on the Hall of the Five Hundreds and one enters the QUARTERS OF ELEONORA FROM TOLEDO, the wife of Cosimo I, prepared especially for her by Vasari (1562). He transformed the halls which were formerly inhabited by the Priors. From a small vestibule in which is a painting of the *Madonna,* attributed to Rossello di Iacopo Franchi, we go into the GREEN HALL, so called on account of the grotesque vault by Ridolfo del Ghirlandaio. At the left is the little STUDIO OF ELEONORA (studio di Eleonora) with the ceiling frescoed by Francesco Salviati. At the right opens the CHAPEL entirely painted by Bronzino (1564) and representing one of the most important works of the artist: at the walls are three stories of Moses depicting *The Crossing of the Red Sea,* the *Bronze Snake* and *Moses who Causes the Water to Spring.* From the Green hall one enters the rooms of Eleonor reconstrueted by Vasari and with the ceilings by Bernardo del Tasso. The frescoes depicting the deeds of famous women, from which derives the very name of the rooms, were painted by Stradano on cartoons by Vasari. The first is the ROOM OF THE SABINES, which was assigned to the ladies of the court; the fresco on the ceiling depicts the *Sabine Women Interposing Themselves among the Romans and the Sabines;* at the walls is a *Madonna and Child,* by Lorenzo di Credi and onother of the same subject by Andrea del Sarto; the various portraits of children of the Medicis, are in the style of Sustermans. Then follows the DINING ROOM or Ester's room, which takes the name from the fresco in the roof depicting *Assuero Crowning Ester,* by Stradano. Very valuable is the washstand in marble of the fifteenth century, and very beautiful are the three arrases with Spring, Autumn and the cart of the Sun. ROOM OF PENELOPE: in the ceiling is *Penelope at the loom* and in the frieze are episodes from the Odyssey; in the walls are two arrases with Summer and Autumn. From the windows one has a magnificent view on the Signoria Square. THE ROOM OF THE BEAUTIFUL GUALDRADA which was the private room of the Duchess: in the vault is *Gualdrada, the Beautiful Daughter of Bellincioni Berti of Adimari,* refusing *to kiss the Emperor Ottone;* in the frieze are views of parties which were given in the main squares and streets of Florence. Through the following passage hall, in which one can note the mask of Dante Alighieri, we enter THE CHAPEL OF THE SIGNORIA. This part of the palace, together with the hall of the Two Hundreds, is what remained

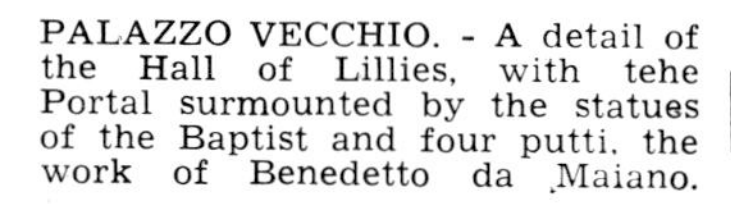

PALAZZO VECCHIO. - A detail of the Hall of Lillies, with tehe Portal surmounted by the statues of the Baptist and four putti, the work of Benedetto da Maiano. ▶

intact of the ancient quarters of the Priors, of the Republican period. In the chapel, Girolamo Savonarola and his companions spent praying the night preceding the execution. The frescoes are by Rodolfo del Ghirlandaio (1514), while the *Sacred Family* on the altar is by Mariotto da Pescia. We pass, then into the halls which were decorated at the period of the Republic. HALL OF THE AUDIENCE, the work of Benedetto da Maiano with the magnificent lacunar ceiling sculptured by Giuliano da Maiano (XV century). At the walls are valuable frescoes by Francesco Salviati (1550-60) depicting *Stories of Camillo's Life*. The very beautiful portal which leads into the following hall, in white marble and porphyry surmounted by the statue of *Fustice*, is the work of Benedetto and Giuliano da Maiano (1476-78); the engraved wooden knickers, in which are depicted Dante and Petrarch ,are by Giuliano da Maiano and Francione (1481). Near-by is the HALL OF THE LILLIES, with the very beautiful portal surmounted by the statues of the *Baptist* and by four putti, the work of Benedetto da Maiano (1476-81). Stupendous also is the lacunar ceiling by Giuliano da Maiano. The decoration of the walls with golden lillies on a blue background (from here comes the name of the hall), commemorates the alliance of the Florentine Republic with Royal House of France. In the wall facing the entrance is a big fresco of feigned architecture by Dominic Ghirlandaio and helpers (1481-85) which from the left depicts *Brutus, Mutius Scevola, Camillus, Saint Zanobi among Lawrence and Stephen, Decio, Scipio, and Cicero*. From the left wall which opens in the wall one can enter the CHANCELLERY, a spacious rectangular hall dedicated to Machiavelli, the Chancellor of the Republic, the photograph of whom is at the wall and is by Santi di Tito (end of the XVI century). There is also a stucco bust in color. At the centre of the hall, over a column, is located the bronze *Winged Genietto and Fish*, a masterwork by Verrocchio (1476) which was found on the fountain of the entrance courtyard and which was transported here for conservation reasons. From the hall of the Lillies, through a door which opens beneath the frescoes by Ghirlandaio, one has access into the MEDICI WARDROBE, also called the hall of geographical maps because on the doors of the cupboards are painted 33 maps attributed to Father Ignazio Danti (1563) the great mathematician and by Don Stefano Buonsignori (1575-84). In the corner at the right of the hall, through a door located between the cupboards, one arrives at the little terrace from which one can observe the ancient part of the palace and to the « little studio » (studiolo) in which Cellini used to go and repair the jewels of the princes. From the grating which is existing to this day, Cosimo I used to spy into the great hall. Once we have come out of the hall of the Lillies, from the door of the right wall, we go into the gallery by means of a staircase; a beautiful panoramic view is possible here. Continuing our ascent up to the top of the tower, we reach the little cell called « alberghetto » (little hotel), in which were put to prison Cosimo the Elder before the exile (1433)and Father Girolamo Savonarola from April 8 to May 23, 1498. In a short while we arrive at the top of the tower from which the panoramic view of Florence and of the surrounding hills is unforgettable.

On the return trip, it is interesting to visit, at the mezzanine, THE LOESER COLLECTION, donated to the city of Florence by the American collector Charles Loeser (d. 1928). The collection includes paintings and sculptures of Tuscan art of the XIV-XVI centuries.

The Uffizi Square.

The Uffizi Square. — Located at the right of the Old Palace, it becomes longer in the pattern of a closed courtyard surrounded by the beautiful and genial construction by Vasari which consists of a porch and a loggia above and the magnificent background with the big arch facing the Arno river. The construction of the imposing building, in which have the headquarters the Gallery of the Uffizi and the State Archives, was commissioned to Vasari by Grand-duke Cosimo I in order to gather there the offices of the government. Begun in 1560, it can be considered the most beautiful architectural work by Vasari, which was completed 1580 by Alfonso Parigi and Bernardo Buontalenti. Towards the middle of the ninenteenth century, in the niches of the external pillars along the arcade, were placed statues of great Tuscans by upside-dom frontispiece and by the bust of Cosimo I. At value with the exception of Saint Antonino, by Giovanni Dupré (1854), and Nicolò Machiavelli by Lorenzo Bartolini (1846). On the corner of Via della Ninna and in the ground rooms of the palace are visible the remains of the Romanesque church of San Piero Scheraggio, of the XI century, demolished on account of requisites of the Vasari construction. The porch at the right of the square is preceded by the ancient palace of the Zecca of which only the ground floor has remained. Under the arch which leads into Via Lambertesca is still the door of the Suppliche (Imploring), an original architecture by Buontalenti, surmounted by upside-dwn frontispiece and by the bust of Cosimo I. At the beginning of Via Lambartesca, at the left, we see the restored house-tower of Pulci, now the headquarters of the ACADEMY OF THE GEORGOPHILES, an old scientific library. Through one of the last doors of the left porch, we enter the STATE ARCHIVES which is specialized in the study of the history of Florence richest collection of documents throughout Italy and a library which is specialized to the study of the history of Florence and of Tuscany. In the show-room are collected precious curios and documents, among which the Fiorinaio or the register of the Money of Florence with the imprint of all golden and silver coins from 1318 to 1859; the diploma of union of the Greek and Latin churches (1439); the book of the nail (chiodo) which contains condemnations of the Ghibellines, among whom are Dante; also, registers, Papal bulls, diplomas, nautical maps, ancient parchments, papyri of the IV-VI century, autographs of humanists, foreign and Medici princes, etc.
From the first door of the left open gallery, flanked by the statues of *Cosimo the Elder « Pater Pariae »* and of *Lawrence the Magnificent*, is the entrance into the Uffizi Gallery.

THE UFFIZI GALLERY

It is world famous for the magnificent and vast collection of paitings of the Florentine and Tuscan schools of the XIV, XV, and XVI centuries.
It also well-known for the great works of the Umbrian, Emilian, and Venetian schools as well as for other Italian schools here represented.
There are also very great works of foreign schools among which the Flemish, the French, and the German. For these reasons this gallery can be considered the most important in Italy and one of the best in the world. The patrimony of the gallery is constituted by the collections of the Medicis and of the Lorrains. It was Granduke Francesco I, a dedicated lover of fine arts, who entrusted Bernardo Buontalenti (1574) to transform the primitive upper arcade, in order to gather in appropriate halls all the works that were scattered in the Palazzo Vecchio and in the Granducal Storeroom and which belonged to Cosimo the Elder, Lorenzo the Magnificent and to Cosimo I. Later Ferdinando I entrusted the same Buontalenti with the construction of the tribune (1610) and had transferred there all the works that he had collected in Rome in the Medici villa. Ferdinand II had new halls added so that works inherited by him from the Della Roveres could be located there. At the same time Cardinal Leopoldo began the collection of self-portraits and of the drawings. Cosimo III donated gems, medals and coins and brought from Rome the famous Venus of the Medicis, the Knife-grinder and other famous sculptures. With Giangastone's death, the last of the Medicis, Anna Maria Lodovica, the wife of Elector Palatine and the last Medici heir, who had already enlarged the precious collection with Flemish and German paintings, donated the whole gallery to the Tuscan State with the « family agreement » of 1737. This agreement said that the rich collection should always remain in Florence. The Lorrains also, continuing the Medici tradition, contributed to the increase of the artistic patrimony: Francesco II of Lorrain donated antiquities and coins and Pietro Leopoldo I, besides gathering the scattered works of the Medicis (in Rome and Florence), brought from the Medici villa in Rome the statues of the Niobides and placed them in a specially built hall. After the spoilations of Napoleon in Italy, the gallery underwent many losses, but, fortunately

The Uffizi Palace.

many if not all of the works were brought back. During the last world war also, despite all precautions taken, many works, some of them of great value, were taken away. This time also, however, Italian authorities have been able to get almost everything back. A well-known example is the two masterpieces by Antonio del Pollaiolo depicting two episodes of the Labours of Hercules (Hercules killing the Hydra and Hercules choking Antheus) which have reappeared after 18 years in America in January 1963 and exactly in Pasadena, California, where the works had been taken by a German couple of American citizenship. The author and editor of this guide wishes to take this opportunity to express to Prof. Rodolfo Siviero, chief of the Italian Committee for the recovery of works of art and to Dr. Luisa Becherucci, the directress of the Uffizi Gallery, personal and heartfelt congratulations on their success in this complex matter of recovering these two art treasures which, thanks to them, once again shine in the halls of the Uffizi Gallery. The present organization of the gallery has been made after the last war, according to the most modern museographical criteria.

Antonio del Pollaiolo: « Hercules killing the hydra » and « Hercules choking Antheus ». (The two masterpieces were recently recovered in Pasadena, California).

UFFIZI GALLERY. - First Corridor.

In the first vestibule, in which entrance tickets are bought, are arranged a few busts of the Medici family. In the second vestibule, in which are visible remains of columns and fragments of frescoes of the pre-existing church of San Piero Scheraggio, is the great portrait of Anna Maria Lodovica, the last of the Medici (d. 1743), by the Flemish painter Sustermans and located here to honour her memory. At the walls are tapestries made by the Medicis and busts of the Medici and Lorrain families. Then follows the great staircase by Vasari along which are arranged sculptures of different epochs, among which very numerous indeed are the Roman copies of Greek originals. On the first floor, on the left is the entrance to the CABINET OF DESIGNS AND PRINTS which is unique in the world on account of the very rich collection begun by Cardinal Leopoldo de' Medici, which consists of over 100.000 samples of Italian and foreign artists. This cabinet is of invaluable help to scholars.

In the first hall are presently shown displays of the individual artists and of schools. On the next floor, besides the six Roman busts, are also two decorative statues in bronze: *Mars* by Ammannati and *Silenus and Bacchus*, a reproduction of the Florentine school of the XVI century of the group which is found in the Vatican. On the second floor we cross the first vestibule decorated with busts depicting personages of the Medici and Lorrain families. From the second vestibule with ancient sculptures we enter the first corridor of the gallery itself.

FIRST GALLERY. — This is the vast loggia which Francis I had transformed by Buontalenti. Along the corridor are disposed numerous sculptures. On the wall is a very beautiful series of tapestries of the XVI century by Florentine and Flemish artists. The decorations on the ceiling with mythological figures are by Allori and other artists of the period (1581).

UFFIZI GALLERY. - **Cimabue:** Madonna in Glory. ▶

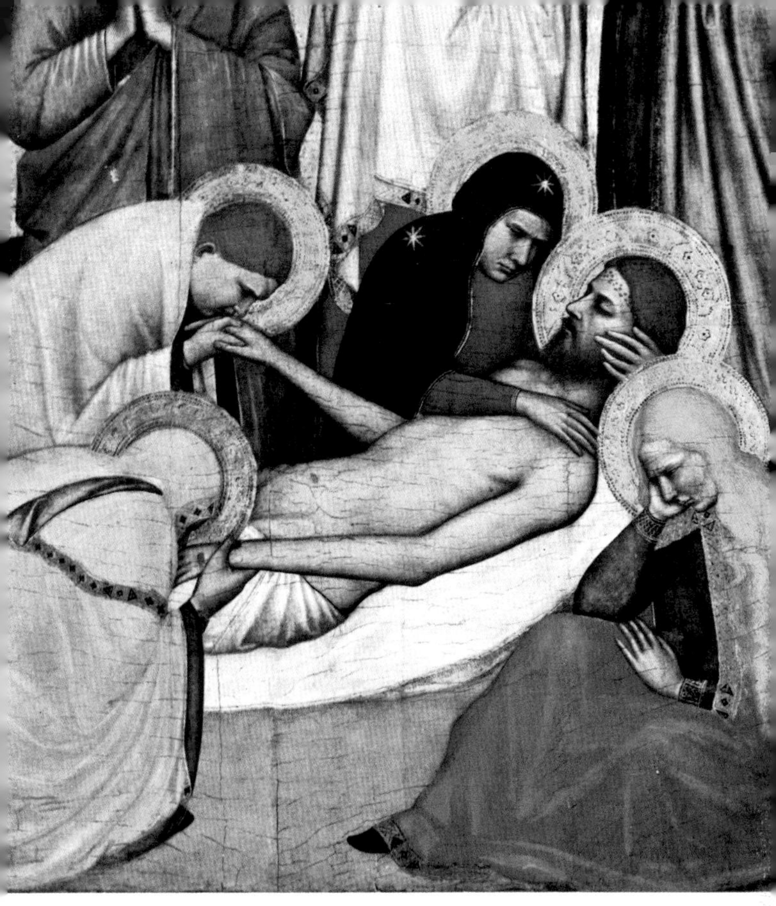

UFFIZI GALLERY. - **Giottino:** Deposition.

ROOM I - (At the beginning of the corridor usually closed). It is also called the hall of Hermaphrodite, because of the statue in the centre of the *lying Hermaphrodite*, a Roman copy of a Hellenist original. On the walls are three Roman copies of the famous bronze sculpture of Doriphorus by Polycleitus. Among the reliefs it is interesting to note the Hellenistic *Resting Wanderer* of the first century A.D. and that of Roman art depicting the *Sacrifice of the Bull*. In the corridor opposite the exit of the hall, is located the marble group of *Hercules killing the Centaur*, a Roman copy of a Hellenistic original, restored in 1595 by Giovanni Caccini.

ROOM II - Dedicated to Italian painters of the XIII century. We meet up with the masterpieces of this century going back to the original sources of Italian painting whenever this, getting away from Byzantine style, became more humane and realistic. *The Madonna enthroned with the Child and Angels*, by Giotto, the authentic initiator of Italian painting, probably carried out in around 1303-1305 in the period in which the artist worked on the frescoes of Assisi. On the lateral walls are another two masterpieces: the *Enthroned*

UFFIZI GALLERY. — **Giotto: « Madonna Enthroned ».**

UFFIZI GALLERY. - **Simone Martini:** Annunciation.

Madonna and Angels by Cimabue (1275) originating from the church of Santa Trinità and the *Enthroned Madonna* by Duccio di Boninsegna (1285), a Sienese painter. The work of the latter is also called Madonna dei Rucellai because it was originally in the Rucellai chapel in the church of Santa Maria Novella. The hall is completed by works of the school of Lucca, among which are the *Stigmata of Saint Francis*, by Bonaventura Berlinghieri. Of notable interest is the *Saint Luke* by the master of the Magdalen and the *Redeemer between the Virgin and Saints Peter and Paul* by Meliore Toscano. Of the Pisan school are the *Crucifix* and the *Stories of the Passion* of the XII century.

UFFIZI GALLERY. - Gentile da Fabriano: Adoration of the Magi.

Room III - It is dedicated to Italian painters of the XIV century. Here are represented the Sienese painters Ambrogio and Pietro Lorenzetti. By the former is *Story of Saint Nicholas from Bari* and the *Presentation of Jesus in the Temple.* By Pietro Lorenzetti are *Stories of the Life of Santa Umiltà*, and a *Madonna and Angels.* By Simone Martini is the famous *Annunciation*, once found in the cathedral of Siena, it is a work of exquisite grace and poetry, a real masterpiece. At the sides are *Saint Ansano* and *Saint Judith* by Lippo Memmi, also a Senese. We also see the *Madonna and Child* by Tozzo Tegiacci; the *Nativity* by Simone dei Crocifissi; the *Presentation in the Temple* by Niccolò Bonaccorsi.

Room IV - In this hall are also found painters of the XIV century, and particularly of the Florentine school, followers of Giotto. By Bernardo Daddi are: the *Madonna and Child*; the *Madonna and Child and Saints*; the *Madonna with Jesus and Angels*; the *Stories of the Virgin.* By Nardo di Cione called Orcagna, is the *Crucifixion.* By Taddeo Gaddi is the *Madonna and Child and Angels.* By Giottino is the original *Descent from the Cross*, which reveals clearly the personality of the painter. By Giovanni da Milano: *Saints; Prophets; Patriarchs; Apostles; Martyrs; Virgins.* In addition there are: the

UFFIZI GALLERY. — **Paolo Uccello:** « Battle Scene ».

Saint Procolo and *Saint Niccolò*, by Ambrogio Lorenzetti and the *Saint Matthew* by Andrea and Iacopo Orcagna.

ROOM V-VI - They are dedicated to Italian painters of the end of the XIV century and the beginnings of the XV century. By Gentile da Fabriano is the beautiful *Adoration of the Magi*, a very colorful, elegant and Gothic work; by the same author are also *Saint Mary Magdalen; Saint Nicholas from Bari; Saint John*; and *Saint George*. By Lorenzo Monaco, also under the influence of a graceful Gothicism, are the *Crowning of the Virgin*, and the *Adoration of the Magi*. By Agnolo Gaddi is: the *Crucifixion*; the *Madonna and Child and Saints Peter and Paul, Thomas of Aquinas and Dominic* is by Giovanni di Paolo. Here is also found the famous Tebaide by Gherardo Starnina.

ROOM VII - Here are collected the masterworks of Italian painting of the XV century. To name a few, the *Madonna and Child*, by Beato Angelico; the *Madonna and Child and Saint Anne* by Masaccio and his teacher Masolino; the famous *Battle of San Romano* by Paolo Uccello. By Filippino Lippi are: *Saint Frediano causes the Serchio to deviate*; the *Angel announces death to the Virgin; Saint Augustine in his studio.* By Domenico Veneziano is the *Madonna enthroned and Saints*, in which are revealed the exceptional talents of this master of colour. There are also the two souvenirs of Piero della Francesca dedicated to *Federico da Montefeltro the duke of Urbino and to his wife Battista Sforza*, with allegorical triumphs of the duke and the duchess behind the panels. Also to be noted is the geometrical stylization of the forms, the vast perspective and the vibrating transparence of the atmosphere.

ROOM VIII - It is particularly dedicated to painters of the XV century: Filippo Lippi and followers. By the master are: the *Madonna and Child and Saints*; the *Crowning of the Virgin*, a rich work with very beautiful portraits of contemporaries: the *Virgin worshiping Her Son and Saint Ilarius*; the *Virgin worshiping Her Son*

UFFIZI GALLERY. — **Masaccio and Masolino:** « Madonna with Child and St. Anne ». ▶

UFFIZI GALLERY. - **Filippo Lippi:** Madonna and Child with Angels.

and Saint Bernard; Madonna and Child and Saints; the *Annunciation; Saint Anthony, Saint John the Baptist.* By the Sienese Lorenzo Vecchietta is the *Virgin and Her Son and several Saints.* By Pesellino, a scholar of Lippi, is the *Miracle of Saint Anthony*; the *Martyrdom of Saints Cosma and Damian*, the *Birth of Christ.* Here is also found the stupendous *Crowning of the Virgin*, by Beato Angelico, Baldovinetti is represented with the *Annunciation* and the *Virgin and Child and Saints.* By Benozzo Gozzoli are: the *Pietà*, the *Saint John* and the *Magdalen.* The *Stories of Saint Benedict* are by the Senese Neroccio di Bartolomeo. By Pietro and Antonio del Pollaiolo are *Saints Vincent, James, Eustace.* By Matteo di Giovanni is the *Madonna and Saints.*

ROOM IX - Here are gathered the works of Sandro Filipepi called Botticelli and of the brothers Piero and Antonio del Pollaiolo. By Botticelli are: the *Fortress*; a *Virile Portrait*; three very beautiful paintings of the *Madonna and Child.* By Piero and Antonio del Pollaiolo there are the *Six Virtues*, and the *Portrait of Duke Galeazzo Sforza.*

ROOM X - It is entirely dedicated to Botticelli, the creator of a harmonious and musical line, and the master who painted elongated figures with the sweetest melancholic expression. There are: the famous *Allegory of Spring* (1478); the *Birth of Venus* (1486); the *Madonna of the Pomegranate*; the *Madonna of the Magnificat* and other masterpieces of his. In the *Adoration of the Magi* (1474), the central group of the Madonna is surrounded by personages of the court of the Medicis: we can recognize there Cosimo the Elder, Piero the Gouty, Lorenzo the Magnificent and others. The figure at the right, turned towards the public, is the painter's self portrait.

ROOM XI - This little hall is dedicated to the small paintings of Botticelli among which the famous *Allegory of Calumny* (about 1495), a late work of the artist. Here is also found the *Madonna Worshiping Her Child* by Filippino Lippi, the pupil of Botticelli, here particularly influenced by the master.

ROOM XII - Here one can find paintings of the Flemish school among which the *Deposition in the Sepulcre* dominates, by Rogier Van der Weyden; the *Madonna enthroned with Angels*, by Hans Memlinc, an artist of acute and subtle psycology and by whom is the *Portrait of a Youth* and the *Portrait of a Man* also, one of the most beautiful works by the master.

ROOM XIII - In this little room are exhibited paintigs by Florentine artists among them: *Allegory*, by Filippo Lippi; *Venus*, by Lorenzo di Credi; *Portrait of an old Man* and *Selfportrait*, youthful works by Filippo Lippi.

ROOM XIV - It is dedicated to Van der Goes, a Flemish painter who had great influence on Florentine painters of the XV century. Here is found the tryptych of the *Adoration*, made after commission of Tommaso Portinari when the artist was in Bruges, around the year 1476, as a Medici agent. At the sides of the triptych are seen portraits of the members of the Portinari family. In this hall are also paintings by Filippino Lippi, Domenico Ghirlandaio and Francesco Botticini who felt the influence of the work of the Fleming.

ROOM XV - It is dedicated to the two major Umbrian painters Luca Signorelli and Pietro Perugino. By Luca Signorelli are the *Sacred Family* and the *Madonna and Child.* By Perugino, the *Madonna between Saints John the Baptist* and *Sebastian.* Here are also found the *Baptism of Christ* (1470) by Verrocchio, the teacher of Leonardo who, as a young man, helped him in the execution of this work, and

UFFIZI GALLERY. - **Sandro Botticelli:** Spring.

UFFIZI GALLERY. - **Ugo van der Goes:** Adoration of the Shepherds.

the paintings of Lorenzo di Credi and of Piero di Cosimo, who were influenced a little by Verrocchio. Here is also the *Adoration of the Magi* by Leonardo, made in 1481, a work which has remained unfinished, but which leaves a quite visible trace of the balanced fantasy of this great genius, through the live expression of his magic chiaroscuro (light and shade).

ROOM XVI AND OF THE GEOGRAPHICAL MAPS - Frescoed in 1589 by Father Stephen Bonsignori with « maps of Tuscany » it is here where the *Annunciation* by Leonardo da Vinci is exposed. This work he did as a young man in the workshop of Verrocchio (1475).

ROOM XVII - Here are more works by Luca Signorelli among which the *Allegory of Fecundity*. There are here other works by Piero di

◀ UFFIZI GALLERY. - **Sandro Botticelli:** Birth of Venus.

UFFIZI GALLERY. - **Leonardo da Vinci:** Adoration (detail).

UFFIZI GALLERY. - **Andrea Mantegna:** Adoration of the Magi.

UFFIZI GALLERY. - **Albrecht Dürer:** Adoration of the Magi.

Cosimo and Lorenzo di Cerdi besides those of Bartolomeo Caporali, Antoniazzo Romano and Giovanni Boccati. To be noted are the two half-figures by Melozzo da Forlì by the title of the *Baptists* and *Saint Benedict*; in the back is the *Annunciation.* This room is temporarily closed for restoration.

ROOM XVIII (TRIBUNE) - It was built by Buontalenti around 1589 to bring together the masterpieces of the Medici collection. In the centre is the famous Greek sculpture of the *Venus of the Medicis*: all around are other Greek and Roman statues. On the walls are portraits by painters of the sixteenth century; they are by Bronzino in most cases and depict personages of the Medicis. Among others are the *Portrait of Eleonora of Toledo* and that of *Lucretia Panciatichi.*

ROOM XIX - Here are found portraits of Perugino beside those of Francia and Costa. The former a Bolognese and the latter a Ferrarese, they were both influenced by Perugino himself. The other works belong to Bolognese and Emilian painters.

ROOM XX - It is dedicated to Andrea Mantegna, the Paduan school principal, and to Alberto Dürer, the great German master from Nuremberg, who was influenced by Mantegna during his stay in Italy. By Mantegna are the famous trjptych with the *Adoration of the Magi* and the beautiful *Madonna of the Caves.* Also by Dürer are an *Adoration* and the *Portrait of his Father* (his first work is dated 1490) Mantegna's influence in Northern Italy is demonstrated by the works of Cosimo Tura of *Saint Dominic* and of Bartolomeo Vivarini with *Saint Ludovico from Tolosa.* The paintings of Luca Cranach among which the *Portrait of Luther and his wife*, the *Portrait of Luther and Melantone*, the *Saint George* and *Adam and Eve*, together with those of his school, complete the picture of Northern painting of the first half of the sixteenth century.

ROOM XXI - It is dedicated to the Venetian fifteenth century, especially to Giovanni Bellini and Giorgione. By the former we see the *Sacred Allegory*, a characteristic work in its almost total unity of colour and the *Pietà of Christ*, painted in chiaroscuro; by the latter, *Moses before the Pharaoh* and the *Judgement of Salomon.* Moreover here are works by Vittorio Carpaccio with the *Group of Armed Men*; by Cima da Conegliano, with a delicate *Madonna and Child*; by Boccaccio Boccaccini, with the *Little Gypsy Girl*, all belonging to the same current. The works depicting *Saint Philip* and *Saint James*, by Alberto Dürer, and the *Virile Portrait* by Hans Burgkmair, recently discovered, are exposed here since they were painted under the influence of Venetian painting.

ROOM XXII - It is dedicated to German and Flemish painters of the sixteenth century among whom: Hans von Kulmback, with the *Stories of Saints Peter and Paul*: Hans Holbein, the great portrait painter, with the *Portrait of Sir. Richard Southwell*; Albrecht Altdorfer, with the *Stories of Saint Florian*; Gerard David, with the dramatic *Adoration of the Magi.*

ROOM XXIII - It is dedicated to Antonio Allegri called Correggio (1489-1534), one of the exponents of Emilian painting of the sixteenth century and in the sphere of Leonardo's influence, for which reason he reached a live personality in the colour and in the grace of the subjects here exposed: the *Adoration of the Child*, the *Rest in Egypt* and the little *Madonna in glory.* Here are also other works by Lombard and Flemish artists more or less influenced by Leonardo.

ROOM XXIV - Here are collected miniatures of Italian and foreign artists from the XV to the XVIII century.

UFFIZI GALLERY. - The second corridor joining the two sides of the building. ▶

UFFIZI GALLERY. — Raphael: « Madonna of the Bullfinch ».

UFFIZI GALLERY. — **Michelangelo:** « Holy Family ».

UFFIZI GALLERY - **Pontormo:** The Supper at Emmaus

SECOND GALLERY. — It joins the two sides of the Uffizi building. Here are found various Roman sculptures among which the *Child removing a Thorn from his Foot; Venus in the Bathroom*; a *Pagan Altar with the Sacrifice of Iphigenia.* From the big windows one can admire the very beautiful view of the Florentine hillside with the picturesque vision of Ponte Vecchio on one side and the porch of the Uffizi and an evocative part of Palazzo Vecchio, on the other side.

THIRD GALLERY. - The corridor is decorated with numerous classical sculptures some of which from the Roman era of the III-IV century A.D.; at the beginning are the two statues of *Marsia* and the *Discus Thrower.* On the left opens the famous corridor built by Vasari in 1564, after commission of Cosimo I, in order to join the Pitti with the Uffizi palace by means of Ponte Vecchio. At the present time, after the disaster of the war, only one part of it has been put to use. It is where has been located the collection of self portraits, this one also is unique in the world. We find Michelangelo, Raphael, Titian, Rubens, David, Vasari, Bernini, Rembrandt, Hayez, Canova. At the back of the corridor, before the terrace on top of the Loggia of the Signoria, is the *Group of Laocoon*, the work of Baccio Bandinelli (XVI century), a copy of the Greek original in the Vatican.

ROOM XXV - Here are exposed works by Raphael and Michelangelo, glories of the Italian sixteenth century. By the former are famous *Madonna of the Goldfinch* (1506); and the very beautiful *Portrait of Pope Leo X with Cardinals Giulio de' Medici* (*the future Pope Clement VII*) *and Luigi de' Rossi* (1518); the *Portrait of Julius II*, which is supposed to be a copy rather than the original. By Michelangelo is one of the very rare paintings by him ever made: the tondo of the *Sacred Family*, called also the Doni tondo from the name of his Commissioner Angelo Doni, who ordered it for his wedding. In this hall are also found a few works of Tuscan and Roman « mannerists », so called because they used to paint in the manner of Raphael and Michelangelo. Of importance are the *Pietà*, by Bronzino and the *Visitation,* by Albertinelli.

ROOM XXVI - Is dedicated to the refined colourist Andrea del Sarto (1486-1531) called « the faultless painter » here present with the *Madonna of the Harpie*s (so called on account of the mythological figures appearing at the sides of the pedestal), and with other important and significant works of his art which lean on chiaroscural design and colouring, the exponent, therefore, of a classical, yet personal, style. The « Mannerists » are here represented by Pontormo and Rosso Fiorentino (let us notice *Moses defending the daughters of Jethro*), Salviati and others.

ROOM XXVII - In the works here exposed is revealed the originality of Iacopo Carrucci called Pontormo (1494-1557), a mannerist also but with an outstanding personality. One of the more interesting of the works here exposed, is the dramatic *Supper of Emmaus*, and among others, the *Madonna and Child between Saint Jerome and Saint Francis* and the *Portrait of Francesco dell'Ajolle.* Another interesting « mannerist » is Bacchiacca by whom we note the *Stories of Saint Ajacio.* The other works are by the Senese Dominic Beccafumi, Rosso Fiorentino and Franciabigio.

UFFIZI GALLERY. — **Titian:** « Venus of Urbino ».

Room XXVIII - Here are found the masterpieces of Titian (1447-1576), who with his marvellous art founded on a luminous and plastic colouring, is the uncontested leader of a century of painting. Among the artist's other works are the famous *Flora*, the also famous *Venus with a Puppy* and the *Portrait of Catherine Cornaro.* Another Venetian, under Titian's influence, is Palma the Elder (1480-1528) who is here present with a few works among which is the *Judith,* of a rich and original colouring.

Room XXIX - It is dedicated to Francesco Mazzola called Parmigianino (1505-40) who presents his masterpiece with the *Madonna with the Long Neck* and the *Portrait of a Man*, held to be his self portrait at one time. Here are also exposed works by French and Emilian painters. To be noted is the *Portrait of a Warrior* by Dosso Dossi, A Ferrarese painter influenced by the Venetians.

Room XXX - The Emilian school is here represented with works of small dimensions among which the *Madonna of Saint Zachariah* by Parmigiano; *Rest in Egypt,* by Dosso Dossi; the *Tribute of the Coin,* by Garofalo.

Room XXXI - It is dedicated to Dosso Dossi, of Ferrarese origin but under Venetian influence. He is represented with works of large dimension: *Witchcraft*; the *Madonna in Glory between the two Saint Johns*; the *Heald of an Old Man.* The *Sick Man* is uncertainly attributed to Sebastiano del Piombo (1485-1547) the Venetian master with a characteristic and luminous colouring, who lived a long time in Rome where he studied Raphael and Michelangelo. By him, however, is the Fornarina, at one time attributed to Raphael.

Room XXXII - It is dedicated to Sebastian del Piombo who is here represented with his major work: the *Death of Adonis.* In this hall

UFFIZI GALLERY. — **Caravaggio:** « Young Bacchus ».

are found numerous works of Venetians of the sixteenth century among which the *Sacred Conversation*, by Lorenzo Lotto; two *Portraits* by Paris Bordone; *Portrait of a Child*, by G. Romanino from Brescia.

Room XXXIII - In this passage corridor (built especially to make easier the passage into the other halls) are gathered works of Italian and foreign artists of the late sixteenth century, among whom Giorgio Vasari, Alessandro Allori, Iacopo Ligozzi, Angelo Bronzino, the Frenchman François Clouet with the *Portrait of Francis I the King of France*, the Spaniard Luis de Morales with *Christ Carrying the Cross*, etc.

Room XXXIV - It is dedicated to Paolo Calieri called Veronese (1528-88), one of the most famous Venetian painters of the sixteenth century for the richness of his composition, for its worth, and for for having been in his paintings the glorifier of the history of Venice in this period. By the artist is exposed in this hall the *Annunciation* and the *Sacred Family with Saint Barbara.* Besides Veronese, here are present Giovan Battista Moroni (1525-78) the great portrait

painter from Bergamo and Giulio Campi from Cremona (d. 1572), both followers of the style of Venetian Masters.

Room XXXV - It is dedicated to the great Iacopo Robusti called Tintoretto (1518-94), with the impetuousness of his painting of a powerful chiaroscuro and of dynamic, dramatic composition. By him are: *Leda and the Swan, Christ and the Samaritan*, a *Portrait of Iacopo Sansovino* and other works. Here is also Iacopo Bassano (1515-92), a very original artist; we see also Federigo Baroccio da Urbino (1528-1612) with the gracious *Madonna of the People* and other works that have some Venetian and Emilian influence.
From Room XXXV one passes into XLI, because rooms XXXVI, XXXVII, XXXVIII, XXXIX and XL have been completely taken apart so as to transform this side of the gallery and precisely for the restoration of the Staircase of Buontalenti. This staircase constitutes the new exit of the gallery, preceded by an elegant vestibule where

UFFIZI GALLERY. — **Tintoretto:** « Leda ».

the *Wild Boar* has been placed (a Roman marble of Hellenistic origins in bronze) from which comes its famous copy in bronze, carried out by Tacca, called « Il Porcellino » (The Little Pig) and which can be found at the Loggia of the New Market. However for your information we can say that Room XXXVI was dedicated to Michelangelo Merisi, known as Caravaggio (1573-1610) the innovator of Italian painting, and creator of an original style with his luminous effects and new realistic-compositive conception. By him *Youthful Bacchus* and the *Sacrifice of Isaac* are exhibited, for the moment anyway, in Room XLI. Some works by other artists that were in the same room, like the *Bacchante* by Annibale Carracci and the *Susanna*, by Guido Reni, are provisorially in Room XXXV. The other rooms contain works by the Dutchman Rembrandt (*Selfportraits* and *Portrait of an Old Man*), Domenico Feti, Bernardo Strozzi, Jacob Ruisdael (*Landscapes*), Gian Battista Tiepolo, Giuseppe Maria Crespi (*The fair at Poggio a Caiano* and *Woman looking for fleas*), Gian Battista Piazzetta (*Susanna and the Elders*), Canaletto with his enchanting views of Venice, Francesco Guardi, Pietro Longhi, Rosalba Carriera, Magnasco (*The Gipsies' Repast*) and others. Many works by these artists are temporarily exhibited on easels in Room XLII.

Room XLII - In this room, known as the Niobe's Room, are exhibited statues of the *Niobes and Niobides*, Roman copies from Greek originals of the III-II century B.C. Moreover works by the French painters Antoine Watteau, Marc Nattier and Chardin, artists of the XVIII century are temporarily exhibited here.

THIRD ITINERAR

PIAZZA DELLA REPUBBLICA - LOGGIA DEL MERCATO NUOVO (NEW MARKET) - VIA POR SANTA MARIA - PONTE VECCHIO - VIA GUICCIARDINI - PITTI SQUARE (PITTI PALACE; PALATINE GALLERY; GALLERY OF MODERN ART; ROYAL APARTMENTS; MUSEUM OF THE HISTORICAL CARRIAGES; SILVER MUSEUM; BOBOLI GARDEN) - VIA ROMANA - VIA MAGGIO - CHURCH OF SANTO SPIRITO - CHURCH OF SANTA MARIA DEL CARMINE (BRANCACCI CHAPEL).

Piazza della Repubblica. (The Republic Square). — It is the modern centre of the city and is located in the same place where once was the old centre of Florence. Demolished in the second half of the nineteenth century, for reasons of hygiene, in order to give rise to the present square, it can now be considered the liveliest place in the city of Florence. On the sides of the square are numerous shops and elegant cafés. The big triumphal arch joins the porches which make up one side of the square and under which is located, on the left, the central post office.

Loggia del Mercato Nuovo. (Loggia of the New Market) — It is located at the end of Calimala Street which begins from Piazza della Repubblica. A Renaissance work by Giovanni del Tasso (1547-51), it is all open by arcades over columns. At one time it was rendered picturesque by the characteristic sale of straws, point laces, laces etc.; for this reason it is known as « the market of the straw ». On the Southern side is the bronze fountain with the wild boar, the work of Pietro Tacca (1612), the replica of an ancient statue which is located in the Uffizi Gallery; the fountain is popularly called « del porcellino » (the little pig's).
Behind the loggia of the New Market, in via di Capaccio, is located the beautiful PALACE OF THE GUELFS an ancient construction of the beginning of the XIV century. Transformed and enlarged at the beginning of the XV century by Brunelleschi (also the author of the facade) it was later completed by Giorgio Vasari to whom we owe the elefant little loggia. In the interior, at the first floor, is a very beautiful hall, which is typical of Brunelleschi, with the wooden roof by Vasari and a work in terracotta by Luca della Robbia, in the lunette.
Coming back and following the side of the loggia as far as Porta Rossa, turning to the left we arrive to the near-by Davanzati square in which rises he DAVANZATI *PALACE*, a typical example of a private home of the fourteenth century and the FORESI TOWER, a characteristic tower-home among the few remained of the 150 which were in Florence in the XIII century and which constituted also a means of civil defense.

Ponte Vecchio (Old Bridge).

PONTE VECCHIO (OLD BRIDGE)

It is so called because it existed at the time of the Etruscans. The first wooden construction, which goes back to 972, was destroyed by the flood of the river in 1333. It was then rebuilt in stone in 1345 by Neri di Fioravante who gave it its present characteristics with the workshops at the sides. At first, these workshops were rented by butchers, but in the XVI century, Cosimo I wanted them to be given to goldsmiths and silversmiths: to this day this tradition is somewhat observed. Above, on the left side, is the famous corridor by Vasari which joins the Uffizi Gallery with the Pitti Palace. In the middle of the bridge opens a double terrace: from the one at the right, where is the *Bust of Benvenuto Cellini* by Raffaele Romanelli (1900), we can enjoy beautiful sight over the bridge of the church of Santa Trinita and of the roads along the Arno; from the one at the left, is a beautiful view of the roads along the Arno and of the hill of San Miniato.

Via Guicciardini. - It is reached after arriving at the Ponte Vecchio. Almost at the beginning on the left, in the homonymous little square, is found the ancient CHURCH OF SANTA FELICITA which has risen over an oratory and Christian cemetery of the V century and rebuilt many times. The present appearance is the work of Ferdinando Ruggeri (XVIII century). The interior, in the form of an Egyptian cross, contains in the first chapel at the right built by Brunelleschi, a beautiful Deposition by Pontormo (1528). In the elegant sacresty of a square plan the work of a follower of Brunelleschi (1470), are valuable paintings among which a *Madonna and Child and Saints*, a polyptych by Taddeo Gaddi and *Santa Felicità and Seven Sons*, a painting with a golden background by Neri di Bicci. In the adjacent chapel with a hemispheric dome, is a painted Crucifix by Pacino di Buonaguida and a *Madonna and Child*, a painting by Giovanni del Biondo. - At the end of Guicciardini's street, on the left, rises the GUICCIARDINI PALACE built at the beginning of the XV century and retouched in the XVII century. The street takes into the huge Pitti square, dominated by the superb structure of the homonymous palace.

PITTI PALACE

This is the most monumental palace in Florence. The construction, designed by Filippo Brunelleschi, goes back to the middle of the XV century and was ordered by Luca Pitti, a very rich merchant who was antagonistic towards the Medici family. He wanted a palace that surpassed all the others in grandeur, and, in addition, had windows as big as the entrance door of the Medici palace in Larga Street(the reference here is to the Medici-Riccardi Palace in Cavour Street). Brunelleschi designed the central part by following his spirit of the Renaissance; namely, balance, simple yet grand forms, three floors of strong ashlar and opened by arcades. In 1465, when the Pittis fell into ruin, the construction was interrupted. In 1549 the palace was bought by Eleonora di Toledo, the wife of Cosimo I, who entrusted Bartolomeo Ammannati with the task of completing the work (1558-70). The great architect knew how to handle his duty without having to change the style of Brunelleschi. In the following century the facade was enlarged by Giulio Parigi (19620) and, later, Alfonso Parigi (the son of Giulio) with ulterior changes brought the facade to its

Pitti Palace.

present appearance. The two lateral wings, called « rondò », were added between 1764 and 1783, after a plan by Giuseppe Ruggeri. The palace, formerly the residence of the Medicis and the Lorenas, gave hospitality to the Royal Family of Savoia in the period in which Florence was the capital of Italy (1865-71). At present here have their headquarters the Palatina Gallery, the Argenti Museum and the Gallery of Modern Art.

COURT-YARD - From the main door we can have access into the majestic, sixteenth-century court-yard by Ammannati (1558-70) who created an incomparable scenery dominated by the CARCIOFO FOUNTAIN, on the above terrace, the work of Antonio Susini and Francesco Ferrucci Junior called Tadda (end of the XVI century). The court-yard has only three complete sides; the fourth forms the terrace the front of which is adorned with two little fountains with *Hercules* and *Anteo* at the left and *Hercules* at the right; the median portal introduces into the the eighteenth-century *Mose's Cave,* with allegorical marble statues.
From the court-yard, through a stairs at the right, we go up to the second floor where we can enter the Gallery of Modern Art (it is advisable to make use of the lift).

Gallery of Modern Art. — Founded in 1860 by the provisional government of Tuscany, it contains works by artists of the XIX century, of the neo-classical and academic periods and of the « macchiaiuolo » movement. The latter was the return to an art which, free from academic convention, found again the source of life and inspiration in the direct contact of reality interpreted with emotive and picturesque synthesis and manifested with sincerity of personal expression. At the head of the « macchiaioli » movement was Giovanni Fattori, with Silvestro Lega, Telemaco Signorini, Giuseppe Abbati, Raffaele Sernesi and others: they are all represented here. Here are found, moreover, the works of contemporary and living artists.

THE PITTI OR PALATINE GALLERY

The gallery consists of 500 paintings, the masterworks of the greatest artists of all time and of superb collections of precious objects to indicate the fabulous wealth of the Medicis and the artistic tradition of this family. For generations and generations the Medicis collected works of art and gave work to artists of all kinds, showing a great sensitivity and such a great passion that Florence was thus able to become the world centre of art which is still very much felt to this day. The original nucleus of the collections goes back to Cosimo II (1620), and, later, by merit of Ferdinand II, it became a superb gallery in which were gathered the works of art brought from Urbino by the wife Vittoria della Rovere. The collection enriched itself later with the intervention of the

PALATINE GALLERY. — Iliad Room.

other Grand-dukes of the Medici and Lorena families. The disposition of the numerous picturesque works located in the luxurious halls decorated with artistic furniture, cloths, vases, etc., is not suggested by historical or museographical criteria, but, rather by decorative intentions.

The big staircase, in typical Brunelleschian style, and by Luigi Del Moro (1897), leads into the vestibule with a magnificent ceiling and decorated by the fountain attributed to Francesco Ferrucci da Fiesole, with the statue of the *Child and Goose,* by Tribolo.

ROOM OF THE ILLIAD (I) - The ceiling is decorated by Luigi Sabatelli (1819) with episodes of the Homeric poem. The central statue in marble depicting *Charity,* is the work of Lorenzo Bartolini (1824). Beginning from the left wall, there is a *Portrait of a Woman called the "pregnant",* by Raffaello (1505); the artist painted it in Florence when he was under the influence of Ghirlandaio; then follows the large picture with the *Assunta* by Andrea del Sarto (1526) by whom is also the other *Assumption of the Virgin* (1519) at the front wall. In the latter painting the artist manifests a fresher inspiration and classical measure in the composition; the *Portrait of a Woman,* by Raffaello del Ghirlandaio, follows and we should note here this artist's influence on Raffaello. At the following wall is a copy of the *Madonna of San Girolamo* by Correggio, done by Baroccio; *The Portrait of a Gentleman,* by Tiziano; *San Filippo Neri in ecstasy,* an imposing cloth painting by Carlo Marotta (Roman school of the XVII century). At the wall facing the entrance: in a corner, are two works by Caravaggio depicting the *Madonna* and *Judith,* by Artemisia Gentileschi. Then follow works by interesting portrait painters of the end of the XVI century and the beginning of the XVII century: Francesco Porbus the Young, Scipio Pulzone and Giusto Sustermans, the official portrait painter of the Medici court by whom is the famous the *Portrait of Valdemaro Cristiano from Danemark,* which is considered his masterpiece, while the famous *Equestrian Portrait of Philip IV of Spain* is by Velasquez.

ROOM OF SATURN (II) - It has the ceiling decorated by Ciro Ferri (1663-65) after a design by Pietro da Cortona. In this room are found many important works by Raffaello. From the left: the famous *Madonna of the Grand-duke* (1505) so called for being the favorite painting of Grand-duke Ferdinand III. Charming indeed is the virginal candor of the Madonna and the timid look of the child who is trying to get a hold of his mother. In this work Raffaello manifests influence of the chiaroscuros of Leonardo and the experiences of the Umbrian school. After the very beautiful composition of the *Dispute of Trinity,* by Andrea del Sarto (1517), is found the *Portrait of Tommaso Inghirami,* the secretary of Julius II, an ancient copy of an original by Raffaello which is found in Boston. Then follow the two portraits by Angelo and Maddalena Doni (1506) by Raffaello by whom is also the little painting with the *Vision of Ezechiello* (1518), which has an influence from Michelangelo, but probaly brought to an end by his pupil Giulia Romano. Above, is the *Madonna by Baldacchino* (1508), the work of Raffaello remained unfinished. Then follow two works by Perugino: the *Deposition from the Cross* (1495) made when the artist had his workshop in Florence and the *Magdalen,* a wonderful work on account of the chiaroscuro. By Fra Bartolomeo is the monumental work with Jesus resurrected *among the Evangelists.* Then follows the *Portrait of Orefice,* by Ridolfo del Ghirlandaio. *The Portrait of the Cardinal Dovizi from Bibbiena,* at the wall before the entrance, is traditionally

PITTI GALLERY. - **Raphael:** « Madonna del Granduca » (detail)

PITTI GALLERY. - **Raphael:** « The Madonna of the Chair.

PITTI GALLERY. - Room of Mars (detail).

SALA MARTE

PITTI GALLERY. - On the left, **Raphael:** « The Veiled Woman » (La Fornarina); on the right, **Andrea del Sarto:** « St. John the Baptist ».

attributed to Raffaello, while by him is the famous tondo with the *Madonna of the Chair* (1515) of his first Roman period and in which is apparent the plastic fullness of the forms: to be observed is the grace with which the Mother hugs Her Son and how San Giovannino also begs for affection. Interesting is the *Saint Sebastian* by Guercino.

Room of Zeus (III) - The ceiling is decorated by Pietro da Cortona and Ciro Ferri (1643-45) with mythological scenes. In the middle of the hall is a marble statue of *Victory* by Vincenzo Consani (1867). On the door is *Christ in the Praetor's Court,* by Iacopo Bassano. At the walls, beginning from the left, is found the restored work of *Saint John the Baptist* (1523), by Andrea del Sarto. Then follows the *Descent from the Cross,* a valuable painting by Fra Bartolomeo, one of his last works and believed to be his masterpiece; *Nymphs attacked by Satyrs,* by Pietro Paolo Rubens; the *Goddesses,* by Rosso Fiorentino, already attributed without any foundation to Michelangelo; *Guidobaldo della Rovere,* a portrait by Bronzino. At the wall that follows is *Saint Mark,* by Fra Bartolomeo; *Annunciation* (1511), by Andrea del Sarto, which is the most beautiful for grace and delicacy among the several made by the artist on the same topic; by him also is the *Madonna and Four Saints,* a work left unfinished at his death. At the wall before the entrance, below, the double portrait is traditionally identified as the self-portrait of Andrea del Sarto and the portrait of his wife. Above, the *Battle,* by Jacques Courtois called Borgognone; then follows the *Portrait of a Woman,* also called the « veiled woman » (1516), a marvelous portrait of the Fornarina whom Raffaello loved until his death and whom we find again in other works such as the *Madonna of San Sisto.* Near the window, is a work by the Venetian School depicting the *Three Ages of Man,* by Giovanni Bellini; above, the *Sacred Family* by Rubens and a *Portrait of a Female,* by Paris Bordone. At the right wall: the *Saviour,* by Baroccio; *Saint Elizabeth* by Guido Reni and, between the window and the door, is the *Madonna and Child,* also called the Madonna della Rondinella, by Guercino.

PITTI GALLERY. - **Pier Paolo Rubens:** « Tre Four Philosphers ».

ROOM OF MARS (IV) - The vault of the hall with *Mars and Hercules* has been frescoed by Pietro da Cortona and Ciro Ferri (1646). On the left is found the masterpiece by Murillo with the *Madonna and Child*, of the Spanish School and another Madonna by the same artist but less valuable than the first. Between the two Madonnas is the work by Rubens of *The Four Philosophers* (1611) in which are depicted the self-portrait of the artist (the first on the left and standing up), his brother Philip, Giusto Lipsio who seems busy explaining a passage which is probably by Seneca whose bust can be seen above; the other is the portrait of Giovanni van Wouver. At the other wall is a *Portrait by Daniele Barbaro* by Paolo Veronese; then follows the great allegorical composition by Rubens (Antwerp 1638) upon commission of Ferdinand II. This work represents *The Consequences of the war,* referring to the Thirty-years war which devastated Europe: here the artist manifests the power of warmth and depth. Then follows the cold *Portrait of Ippolito de' Medici* by Tiziano and by him also is the following *Portrait of Andrea Vesalio.* The *Portrait of Cardinal Bentivoglio,* at the wall before the entrance, is a masterpiece by Antonio van Dick (1623) of very live effects and one of the best portraits existing in this gallery. Then follow the *Portrait of Luigi Cornaro* by Tintoretto and *Saint Peters in Tears* by Guido Reni. At the right wall is the *Conception* by Luca Giordano and right of the door a beautiful Saint Sebastian by Guercino.

Room of Apollo (V) - In this room also the ceiling has been frescoed by Pietro da Cortona and Cirro Ferri (1647-60). Above the door is the *Madonna of the Pity* by Tiziano. At the entrence wall is *The Man with Gray Eyes,* one of the most famous portraits by Tiziano containing a mysterious fascination; *Portrait of Vincenzo Zeno,* a superb masterpiece by Tintoretto; then follow two works by Andrea del Sarto with the *Holy Family* and the imposing *Deposition*; beneath, *a Nymph chased by a Satyr,* by the Ferrarese Dosso Dossi. At the following wall: *Saint John the Baptist* by Dosso Dossi; a *Portrait of Frederic, the Prince of Urbino, as a Young Man* is by Baroccio; *Madonna and Saints* is a masterpiece by the mannerist painter Rosso Fiorentino; *Saint Peter Resuscitates Tabita,* by Guercino. At the wall before the entrance is another subject with the *Holy Family* by Andrea del Sarto; *Hospitality of San Giuliano* by Cristoforo Allori; a double portrait of *Charles I of England and Henrietta of France,* by Antonio van Dick. At the right of the entrance is the *Magdalen* by Titian and the self-portrait of Andrea del Sarto.

Room of Venus (VI) - The vault is frescoed by Pietro da Cortona helped by Ciro Ferri and decorated with valuable stuccos by Roman artists (1641-42). On the left wall is found the famous *Portrait of a Gentlewoman* called « the beautiful », by Titian who probably has made a portrait of Duchess Eleonora Gonzaga of Urbino. Then follows the *Sacred Conversation* by Bonifacio de' Pitati called Bonifacio Veronese; *Marina* by Salvator Rosa; *Portrait of Pietro Aretino,* a late work by Titian. At the following wall are two works by Rubens: *The Return of Farmers from work and Ulysses at the Island of the Phaecians.* Then follow the *Martyrdom of Saint Catherine* by Francesco Bassano and *Apollo and Marsia* by Guercino. At the wall before the entrance is a *Portrait of Julius II* once attributed to Raffaello, but presently certainly a work by Titian from the original work by Raffaello preserved in the Uffizi Gallery. The successive work represents the famous *Concert,* once attributed to Giorgione, but in reality, it is the early work of Titian (1518) when he was still under the influence of the art of Giorgione: very expressive indeed is the lost look of the the friar sitting on the clavicembolo looking towards the lute player. At the right wall is the *Apparition of Jesus to Saint Peter* by Gigoli.
From this hall we can go into the Royal flats but it is advisable to end the visit to the halls of the Palatine Gallery by going through the door at the left wall.

Castagnoli Room (VII) - Its name derives from the painter who decorated it in the XIX century. In the middle is a large circular table called « of the Muses » with the flat portion in hard stones of Florentine manufacture (1851) with Apollo at the centre and the symbols of the Muses all around; the supporting leg is in bronze with the seasons and puttis and is by Giovanni Dupré (XIX cent.). At the right is a magnificent banner by Sodoma painted in 1525 for a fraternity from Siena: in the front portion is depicted the *Martyrdom of Saint Sebastian*, in which the artist shows his charm for the works by Leonardo; behind the banner is *The Madonna and Child in Glory and Saints*. At the left the painting of very lively colors depicting *Bacchus* is the work of Guido Reni.

Through the door at the right, before the entrance, we enter the ROOM OF ALLEGORIES (VIII) also called « of Volterrano » on account of the frescoes with allegories by Baldassare Franceschini called Volterrano. This hall contains works by Florentine artists. In the successive ROOM OF THE ARTS (IX), with the ceiling devanni, the magnificent Florentine artist of the XVII century. - and the *First Night in a Honeymoon* by Giovanni da San Gio- *Madonna and Child* by Artemide Gentileschi; *Venus and Love* painters of the XVII century, among which *The Jest of the Rector Arlotto, Venal Love* and *Sleeping Love*, by Volterrano; *Madonna and Child*, by Artemide Gentileschi; *Venus and Love* and *First Wedding Night*, by Giovanni da San Giovanni, the magnificent Florentine artist of the XVII century. In the following ROOM OF THE ARTS, with the ceiling decorated with a fresco of the Mayor (XIX), continues the series of the works by Florentine painters of the XVII century among whom Cristoforo Allori with the *Adoration of the Magi;* Cigoli with the *Stigmata of Saint Francis;* Dolci; Ligozzi; Rustici, etc. - Then follows the ROOM OF HERCULES (X), decorated by the painter Pietro Benvenuti (1828) in neo-classical style. At the centre is the magnificent *Vas of Sevres* given as a present to Ferdinand III by Napoleon. - ROOM OF DAWN (XI) with the ceiling decorated by G. Martinelli (XIX century). Here are collected work by Florentine artists of the XVII century. Lorenzo Lippi with the *Triumph of David;* Empoli with *Dead Nature;* Giorgio Vasari; Sustermans; Fontana and others. - ROOM OF BERENICE (XII), with the ceiling decorated by Giuseppe Bezzuoli (XIX century). Here are exposed works by the Neapolitan Salvator Rosa among which *Marina;* the *Broken Bridge;* the *Battle;* the *Forest of the Philosophers*. - (The five halls that follow are actually closed for repairs).

Returning into the Castagnoli Hall (VII), from the door that opens at the left wall opposite the banner of Sodoma, we enter the ROOM OF MUSIC OR OF THE DRUMS (XVIII), so called on account of the original shape of the small furniture here located. The frescoes are by Luigi Ademollo. Among the paintings, *Cleopatra* is the restored work by Guido Reni; *Portraits of Females*, by Pontormo; *Annunciation*, by Baroccio; the three portraits are by Giovanni and Francesco Clouet. The table at the centre of the hall is of malachite from Russia and supported by a gilded bronze structure (1819).

POCCETTI GALLERY (XIX) - It takes its name from the sixteenth century painter who frescoed the vault. Here are exposed works by artists of the XVII century. At the entrance hall, at the sides of the door, are two portraits by Rubens and works by Francesco Furini, with *Ila and the Nymphs;* Giuseppe Ribera called the Spagnoletto (Little Spaniard), with the *Martyrdom of Saint Bartholomew;* Gaspare Dughet called Paussin, with four *landscapes;* Domenico Feti, with the Lost Drachm; the artist Schiavone, with the *Adoration of the Magi;* Salvator Rosa with a self-potrait.

ROOM OF PROMETHEUS (XX) - In the vault and high in the walls are frescoes with *Stories of Prometheus*, by the Florentine Giuseppe Collignon (1842). At the left wall: the *Holy Family* by Iacopo del Sellaio; the *Martyrdom of 11.000 Crowned Martyrs* by Pontormo; the *Holy Family* by Mariotto Albertinelli; the same

PITTI GALLERY. - **Filippo Lippi**: Madonna and Child.

◀ PITTI GALLERY. - **Tizian**: « La Bella ».

subject by F. Granacci; *Madonna of the Roses* from the School of Botticelli; the *Holy Family* by Beccafumi; the *Madonna and Child and Angels* by Botticini: the Holy Family by Luca Signorelli. At the hall facing the entrance: the *Calumn of Apelle* by Franciobigio; the *Madonna and Child*, a big tondo by Filippo Lippi (1452) with the birth of the Virgin and the meeting of Anna and Gioacchino at the golden gate in the background; *Dance of Apollo with the Nine Muses* by Giulio Romano; the *Holy Family* by Granacci; the *Holy Family and Angels* by Botticelli; *Ecce Homó.* by Fra Bartolomeo; Magdalen by Bachiacca. At the right wall: the Holy Family by Domenico Poligo. - From the corner at the right of this hall we go into the CORRIDOR OF THE COLUMNS (XXI), which takes its name from the two columns in Oriental alabaster. Here are exposed Flemish and German paintings of small dimensions of which worthy of attention are the *Views*, by Cornelius Poelenburg and the *Alchemist* by David Teniers the Elder. At the right wall is the *Virgin in Sorrow* a chiaroscuro by Antonio van Dyck.

ROOM OF JUSTICE (XXII) - The allegorical decorations of the ceiling are by Antonio Fedi (1830). In this hall are mainly collected works of the Venetian School of the VI century of which of importance are: at the entrance wall, *San Giacomo Maggiore* by Garofalo, a copy of the original by Dosso Dossi; *Baptism of Christ* by Paolo Veronese; *Venus, Vulcano and Love* by Tintoretto. At the right wall: *Moses saved from the waters* by Bonifacio de' Pitati who got inspiration from Giorgione; *Portrait of a Gentleman* by Titian. At the wall before the entrance: the Redeemer, an early work by Titian unfortunately restored: *Madonna and Child* and *two Portraits* by Tintoretto, *Augustus* and *Sibilla* by Bonifacio de' Pitati; a *Portrait by Tommaso Mosti* by Titian.

ROOM OF FLORA (XXIII) - The frescos on the vault are by Antonio Marini (1830). In the middle of the hall, *Venus Italica*, a marble statue of perfect form by the neo-classical artist Antonio Canova, a gift of Napoleon to substitute the Venus of the Medicis brought to Paris, which was returned in 1815 and placed in the Uffizi Gallery. Here are mainly collected works of Florentine painting of the XVI century. At the entrance wall: a *Portrait of Luca Martini*, by Bronzino; *Adoration of the Magi* by Pontormo; the *Holy Family* and *Portrait* by Michele di Ridolfo del Ghirlandaio. At the right wall: *Portrait* by Salviati; *Martyrdom of Saint Agatha* by Sebastiano del Piombo. At the wall facing the entrance: *Madonna and Child* by Puligo; *Stories of Saint Joseph* by Andrea del Sarto.

ROOM OF THE PUTTI (XXIV) - In this room also the ceiling is decorated by Antonio Marini. Here are found paintings of the Flemish and Dutch Schools with subjects for the most part of dead natures, landscapes and sea-pieces. Of the greatest value is the *Vase of Flowers* by Giovanni van Huijum; *Flowers and Fruit* by Rachele Ruisch; *Marina* (sea-piece) by Enrico Giacomo Dubbles; *The Three Graces*, a monochrome by Rubens.
Returning into the Room of Promotheus (XX), through the door at the right we have access into the other rooms.

ROOM OF ULYSSES (XXV) - The fresco in the ceiling depicting the *Return of Ulysses to Ithaca*, a mediocre work by Gaspare Martellini, wants to symbolize the return of Ferdinad III to Tuscany, after the Restauration. Entrance wall: at the door is a *Portrait of Alfonso from Ferrara* attributed to Titian; *Madonna dell'Impannata*, so called because the window is clased by an « impannata » (window filled with paper or cloth), a work attributed to Raffaello but which is presumed to have been made by one of his pupils after the maestro designed it. At the left all: *Madonna and Saints* an imposing early composition by Andrea del Sarto;

PITTI PALACE. - Museo degli Argenti.

Death of Lucretia by Filippino Lippi; *Epiphany*, of the Umbrian School of the XV century; *Artificial Love* by Orazio Riminaldi. At the wall facing the entrance are various works by Carlo Dolci among which the very beautiful Magdalen and the famous work by the Florentine painter Cigoli depicting *Ecce Homo*. In addition there is the *Portrait of Andrea Frizier* by Tintoretto.

SMALL BATHROOM (XXVI) - In neo-classical style by Giuseppe Cacialli, it is decorated with stuccos and basreliefs.

ROOM OF THE EDUCATION OF ZEUS (XVII) - It takes its name from the subject of the fresco in the ceiling by Luigi Catani (1819). At the entrance wall: on the door, *The Chaste Susanna* by Guercino; *Pietà* by Francesco Salviati; *Giuditta* by Cristoforo Allori - this represents his masterpiece: It is said that the head of Oloferne is the self-portrait of the artist who grew a beard for this reason: *Saint Sebastian* of the Bolognese School of the XVII century. At the left wall is an interesting *Portrait of a Man* by Antonio van Dyck. At the wall before the entrance are the masterpieces of Caravaggio: *Sleeping Love, Rest in Egypt* by Bonifacio de' Pitati and works of the School of Paolo Veronese.
ROOM OF THE STOVE (XXVIII) - It is so called because it is exposed to the sun. *Allegory* of Fame in the vault, *Strength* and *Prudence* and *Justice* and *Charity* in the pennacchi and the *Four Great Monarchies* in the lunettes are all frescos by Matteo Rosselli (1622). The *Four Ages of Humanity*, at the walls, are frescos by Pietro da Cortona (1637-40).

Here ends the visit to the rooms of the Palatine Gallery. Returning into the room of Venus (VI), through a door at the left, we enter the ex-royal flats.

Ex - Royal Apartments. - Once the residence of the Medicis and the Lorenas, it became later the residence of the Savoias. The first is the DINING ROOM (also called hall of the Niches), with portraits of Medici personages by the court painter Sustermans. At the walls are Japanese and Sevres vases. Then follow the GREEN ROOM with arrases of Gobelins manufacture and with frescos by Luca Giordano with allegorical subjects in honour of the Medicis. - ROOM OF THE THRONE with portraits by Sustermans and Francesco Porbus and magnificent vases in majolica. The throne under the canopy was used for the oath ceremony of the kings of Italy. - BLUE ROOM, with Gobelins arrases, portraits by Sustermans and very beautiful Chinese vases. - CHAPEL, which was changed into a hall after 1865. - ROOM OF THE PARROTS, so called on account of the motifs in the tapestry. At the walls is the *Portrait of the Duchess of Urbino* by Titian and the *Portrait of Francesco I* by Hans von Aachen. This hall with the following two formed the quarters of Queen Margaret and more precisely the YELLOW ROOM with Gobelin arrases and portraits among which that of the *Elettrice Palatina* attributed to J.F. Douven and the bed-room of the Queen with very beautiful furniture of imperial style. Returning into the Room of the Parrots we go into the flat of King Umberto I. The bed-room, the studio and the halls are decorated with arrases and portraits, while the ROOM OF BONA is decorated with frescos by Poccetti (XVII century) depicting the *Conquest of the City of Bona in Africa*, the *Conquest of Prevesa*; *View of the Harbour of Livorno*; *Apotheosis of Cosimo I*. - THE WHITE ROOM also called the BALL ROOM with magnificent ne-classical stuccos and very beautiful chandelier. In this hall, during the stay of the Lorenas and the Savoias, took place receptions and ceremonies.

After the visit to the Palatine Gallery and the Royal Flats is over, we return to the main floor to visit the Silver Museum which we can enter through the same entrance of the Palatine Gallery,

Silver Museum. — It is one of the richest collections of silver, precious stones, jewels, ivories, porcelains, glasses, cloths, etc.. This collection, of infinite value, belonged to the Medici family. It was later increased from the treasures of the Elettrice Pala-

PITTI PALACE. - Royal Apartments: Sala delle Nicchie.

tina, from donations of the Savoias and from privates. It would take much room to list the objects and works that are found in the halls, thus, as has been done for ather museums and galleries, only the things of greatest interest will here be cited.

ROOM I - It is decorated with frescoes by Michelangelo Colonna and Agostino Mitelli (1640-44). At the walls are ancient marble busts. Opposite the window is a very beautiful cabinet in ebony and hard stones of the XVIII century with an urn of the Elettore Palatino Giovanni Guglielmo, the last of the Medicis and husband of Anna Maria Lodovica. In the central windows are gilded silver cups, the works of Vavarian goldsmiths of the XVI-XVII centuries. On the table in porphyry in the middle of the hall is a marble group with *Sleeping Putti*, a sculpture of the School of Bernini. At the left all is a faldstool in ebony and mosaics. In the corner is a large silver plate with the *Madonna and the Misteries of Rosary*. At the other side is a bronze Crucifix of the School of Giambologna.

ROOM II - Decorated with frescoes by Michelangelo Colonna and Agostino Mitelli (1649). In the first window at the left is *Mitre and Mexican Lappets* embroidered with feathers of birds (Mexican art of the XVI century). In the other windows are mainly found works by Bavarian goldsmiths of the XVI-XVII centuries.

ROOM III - It was decorated by Colonna and by Mitelli. The *Cabinet of Alemagna*, placed at the center of the hall and containing a little altar, is the place for sacred objects and sacred statuettes in hard stone and belonged to to Cardinal Leopoldo de' Medici. It is said he celebrated the holy mass here.
In the passage way that follows, at the left is a small chapel with *Crucifixes* and *Silver Chandeliers* by goldsmiths from Hapsbourg.

ROOM IV - It is decorated with frescos by Giovanni da San Giovanni and helpers (XVII century), depicting allegories that exalt the mecenatism (patron of the arts, letters, etc.) of Lorenzo de' Medici. In the second central window is a crystal *Cup* with a cover in gold and arabesque designs with the coat-of-arms of Henry II of France and of Diana from Poitiers. In the same window are valuable works in hard stones and glass of Florentine manufacture of the XVI century. In the third window are ancient vases and jaspers belonging to Lorenzo de' Medici and a *vase* in lapislazzuli (precious stone so named) made after a design by Buontalenti and for Francesco I de' Medici (1583). Among the marble busts along the walls, to be noted is that of *Marie Antoinette*, the Queen of France, attributed to G. A. Houdon.

ROOM V - At the walls are arrases of Florentine manufacture of the XIV and XVII centuries with episodes of the life of Clement VII de' Medici and of Grand Duke Cosimo I. In the windows, under and opposite the windows, are precious pieces in hard stone also destined for the altar of the Princes Chapel in San Lorenzo, but which was nover brought to completion. To be noted are the eight *Statuettes of Apostles* in hard stones and made by Orazio Mochi; the panel in hard stones, gold and jewels depicting *Cosimo II in Prayer*, designed by Bilivert and made by Orazio Mochi; a large cameo (stone cut in relief) with the *Family of Cosimo I*, engraved by G. Antonio de Rossi (XVI century).

ROOM VI - The decoration of the ceiling is of the XVII century. Under the window is a gracious fountain with putti of the XVII century. In this hall are contained the Medici collections of gems, cameos and jewels belonging to the Elettrice Palatina.
Having returned in the third hall in which is the cabinet of Alemagna, we enter the other rooms.

BOBOLI GARDENS. — Giambologna: « Fountain of the Ocean ».

ROOM VII - It contains precious works in amber.

ROOM VIII - In this hall are collected cloths, arrases, embroidered works, rugs and sacred objects of the XV-XVI centuries. Of special interest are the pluvial embroidered in silk, silver, gold and precious stones, with the *Crowning of the Virgin*, the work of Iacopo Cambi (XIV century), originating from Santa Maria Novella.

ROOM IX - Among the various arrases of this hall, notable is the Flemish one of the XVI century depicting the *Baptism of Christ*. In the shop windows are seen ivory works and other things.
Returning into the passage way between the IX and the VIII room we reach the MEZZANINE where are collected in numerous halls precious majolicas and porcelains manufactured in Vienna, Chelsea, Capodimonte, Saxony, Sèvres and Ginori. In the last hall is found the *Portrait of Napoleon* in porcelain from Sèvres.
Once we have ended the visit to the Silver Museum, we complete the visit in Palazzo Pitti by visiting the Boboli garden.

THE BOBOLI GARDEN

It is so called because it rose on the hill which was called in this way. It is a wonderful garden in the Italian style; that is to say, it follows a certain architectural concept. The garden was wanted by Eleonora of Toledo, the wife Cosimo I, who entrusted Niccolò Pericoli called Tribole (1542) with the work. It was then continued by Ammannati and Buontalenti and finally by Alfonso Parigi.

Right on the left is the *Fountain of Bacchino*, a ràther bizarre figure which represents the court dwarf of Cosimo I. In the fackground opposite the entrance gate, is found the *Cave of Buontalenti*, a fantastic whole of artificial caves decorated with frescos, sculptures and false incrustations. In the first cave the tomb of Julius II, and now substituted by counter-drawings. In the third cave is found the beautiful *Venus of the Little Cave* by Giambologna. Returning to the entrance square, the street at the right leads into the Anphitheater, an eighteenth-century construction with the central basin in granite originating from the Terme di Caracalla (Warm Baths of Caracalla) in Rome and surmounted by an Egyptian obelisk. From the back of the Anphitheater we go up to the TANK OF NEPTUNE which derives its name from the bronze statue in the middle of the basin, representing the *God of the Sea* by Stoldi. From here, towards the left, we have access into the BELVEDERE from where we can enjoy a beautiful view of the panorama and of the surrounding hills.
Returning to the large basin we go up as far as the *Statue of Abundance*, the work of Giambologna and Tacca and, turning to towards the right, we reach the GARDEN OF THE KNIGHT with a very beautiful view of the surroundings. Coming down from the staircase way in the back at the left is the meadow surrounded by cypress trees and tit-bits and called the MEADOW OF THE BIRDS. From here begins the stupendous and long avenue which leads to the SQUARE OF THE ISLAND with the *Fountain of the Ocean* at the centre by Giambologna. Thus, passing through the « LIMONAIA » (lemon orchard) we reach the exit which takes into Via Romana.

Via Romana. — From the gate exit of the Boboli garden we enter Via Romana. The itinerary continues by turning to the right.
(If we turn left instead, the street leads to Porta Romana, a bold, massive construction of 1326. In the interior, above the arch, is a fresco by Franciabigio depicting the *Madonna and Child and Four Saints*. From Porta Romana Square, at the left begins Machiavelli Avenue, a splendid promenade which leads to Piazzale Michelangelo. Further on the right goes up the Avenue of Poggio Imperiale flanked by tit-bits, cypress trees and pines which leads to the Villa of Poggio Imperiale, an ancient construction enlarged in 1620 by Giulio Parigi and retouched many times in the future. At present, it is the headquarters of the SS. Annunziata Institute for Women. Coming back to Via Romana on the facade of the first house we see the great modern fresco (1955) depicting the *Life of Florence,* the work of the Florentine painter Mario Romoli. This work substitutes that of the eighteenth century by Giovanni da San Giovanni which has been lost. Both ancient and modern personages are arranged in a typically Florentine architectural environment. In the middle above the little window is the *Annunciation;* at the right great persons who honoured the city: Dante, Giotto, Masaccio, Leonardo, Michelangelo, Savonarola and Giovanni dalle Bande Nere; at the left the figure with eyeglasses is the writer Giovanni Papini; then, we see the self-portrait of the painter, the Mathematician and Professor Campedelli, architect Italo Gamberini and the figure with the little statue in its and which is sculptor Martini).
Continuing the itinerary from the exit of the Garden of Boboli, at No. 17 of Via Romana, has its headquarters the MUSEUM OF PHYSICS AND NATURAL HISTORY more commonly called the Specola. At the end of the street we arrive in San Felice Square where at the left is the CHURCH OF SAN FELICE with Michelozzo's facade (1457) and the very beautiful, carved Renaissance Portal. The interior, with only one nave, contains valuable works of art among which at the first altar the *Pietà* by Nicolò di Pietro Gerini (XIV century); at the fifth altar is a *Madonna and Child and Saints* by Ridolfo del Ghirlandaio; at the seventh altar on the left is *San Massimo helped by San Felice* by Giovanni da San Giovanni. At the wall of the chorus is a Crucifix from the workshop of Giotto.

Via Maggio. — It is a perfectly straight street which begins from San Felice Square and it is so called because, originally, it was called Major Street on account of its great size. It is flanked by aristocratic palaces built in the XIV and XVII centuries. We reach the centre by crossing the bridge of Santa Trinità. At the beginning at No. rises the home of Guidi in which lived and died (1861) the famous English Poet Elizabeth Barrett Browning; here we notice an epigraph above the door dictated by Niccolò Tommaseo in honour of the author. At No. 26 is the sixteenth Palace of Buontalenti in which lived Bianca Cappello, the lover of Francesco de' Medici. Of the other palaces, those worthy of attention are: at No. 43 the home of Ridolfi (XIV); No. 50 the home of Rosselli del Turco (XV century); No. 42 the Corsini Palace (XV century) retouched by G. Silvani; No. 30 the Biliotti Palace.
Returning to San Felice Square, the short Mazzetta Street leads to the picturesque Santo Spirito Square, in which right on the right at No. 10 rises the GUADAGNI PALACE, a very beautiful example of a Renaissance Florentine Palace (1503-06) with two orders of arched windows and attributed to Cronaca; above is a beautiful loggia and an iron lantern at the corner.

CHURCH OF SANTO SPIRITO. — Interior.

CHURCH OF SANTO SPIRITO

Rising on the spot in which was a thirteenth century little church annexed to the Convent of Augustin, it is among the purest creations of the architecture of the first part of the Renaissance. Begun in 1444 by Brunelleschi, it was then continued by Antonio Manetti and Salvi di Andrea and finished in 1487. The slim bell-tower on the left side is by Baccio d'Agnolo. The dome was built by Salvi d'Andrea after a design by Brunelleschi. Beautiful, in the simplicity of its lines, the right flank.

THE INTERIOR, elegant with its light arches and slim columns, is in the shape of a Latin cross with three naves which continue also in the transept. The 38 semi-circular chapels were rich of works of art at a time, but were later removed for the most part. Right nave: in the II chapel is found the Pietà, a copy of the original by Michelangelo which is found in the Church of Saint Peter in Rome, built by Baccio Bigio (XVI century). In the III chapel is a wooden statue by *San Niccolò da Tolentino* attributed to Nanni Ungaro. In the VI chapel is the *Martyrdom of Santo Stefano* by Passignano. Behind the Baroque Major Altar (1608) with the sumptuous tabernacle made after a design by Giovanni Caccini, is a wooden *Crucifix* attributed to twenty-year-old Michelangelo. Right transept: in the IV chapel, on the

CHURCH OF SANTA MARIA DEL CARMINE. - **Masaccio:** « Payng of the Tribute Money » (Brancacci Chapel).

altar of the XV century, is a *Madonna and Child, San Giovannino and Saint,* also called the Virgin of the Tanai Family; let us notice also a work by Filippo Lippi (1490) with a beautiful representation of his period. In the VII chapel, behind the marble-like bronze grating, is a *Sarcophagus by Neri Capponi* by Bernardo Rossellino (1458). Apse: In the I chapel is a *Madonna and Saints*, a work attributed to Raffaello de' Carli. In the II chapel, is a *Madonna and Child and Saints* of the School of Bernardo Daddi. In the IV chapel is the *Martyr Saints* by Alessandro Allori. In the bridle is a view of the Pitti Palace before its enlargement. In the V chapel is the *Adulteress,* by Alessandro Allori. In the VII chapel is the *Annunciation* of the Florentine School of the XV century. In the VIII chapel is the *Nativity* of the School of Ghirlandaio. At the left transept we can see how has been kept the whole of the fifteenth century. In the first chapel is *Santa Monica Founding the Order of the Augustinians,* by Botticini. In the II chapel is a *Madonna and Child and Saints,* by Cosimo Rosselli (1482). In the IV chapel the whole decoration in marble is the early work of Andrea Sansovino. Interesting also is the altar rail of 1642. In the V chapel is the *Holy Trinity* by Francesco Granacci. In the VII chapel is a *Madonna and Child and Saints* by Raffaellino del Garbo (1505). In the VIII chapel is the *Incredulity of Saint Thomas* by Michele del Ghirlandaio. At the VI chapel is Christ Carrying the Cross, a copy of the original by Michelangelo in Saint Mary above Minerva in Rome, made by Taddeo Landini. From the door under the organ, at the third span, we have access into the VESTIBULE with a barrel vault supported by twelve Corynthian columns and built by Cronaca (1494). This precedes the beautiful SACRESTY in an octagonal plan, built after a design of Giuliano da Sangallo; the dome was finished in 1497 on a model of Antonio del Pollaiolo and Salvi d'Andrea.

Cenacolo of Santo Spirito. — The entrance is on the left of the facade of the church. Here are collected Medieval and Renaissance sculptures (from the XI to the XV centuries) given to the city of Florence by the Collectionist Salvatore Romano. At the wall of the great hall, once a refectory of the Augustinians, is an imposing fresco with the *Last Supper* and *Crucifixion* by Andrea Orcagna and helpers (1360). At the other walls are frescos of the XIV century.

Crossing the square again at the right is Saint Augustine Street at the end of which , after crossing the Via dei Serragli, is Via Santa Monaca which takes in a short time to del Carmine Square.

CHURCH OF SANTA MARIA DEL CARMINE

Built in 1268 in Gothic-roman style, it was many times restored in the XV-XVII centuries. In 1771 it was almost entirely destroyed by a fire from which were miraculously seved the Corsini and Brancacci chapels. It was then rebuilt by Giuseppe Ruggeri and Giuliano Mannaioni (1771-75) in style of the period. The facade has remained unfinished.

THE INTERIOR is in the shape of a Latin cross with only one nave in which are various chapels. The vault is frescoed by Domenico Stagi with artificial architectures. The big fresco depicting the *Ascent is* by Giuseppe Romei (1780). At the third altar on the right, is a picture with *Jesus Crucified,* the *Madonna, the Magdalen, and Saint John,* the work of Vasari which escaped the fire of 1771. Back of the right arm of the cross-vault, opens the BRANCACCI CHAPEL, miraculously escaped from the fire, in which is found the famous cycle of Felice Brancacci who had built the chapel. The frescos were then continued by Masaccio (1426-27) and finally completed by Filippino Lippi (1484-85). - Masaccio was the great innovator of the fifteenth century who brought art to a human conception, adherent, that is to say, to a real vision, in which situations and sentiments acquire a dramatic value and the the figures appear powerfully blocked in their monumentality. In his brief life, as he died when he was hardly twenty-eight (1401-28), Tommaso Guidi called Masaccio, brought with his expressive power a real revolution in the field of art and influenced in this way successive generations. The actual period also has taken from this great maestro its lesson. The decoration of the chapel of the Brancacci family was entrusted to Masolino da Panicale, who is presumed to be Masaccio's teacher, but who has some Gothic in him and paints figures that are full of grace with a pleasant and narrative taste. Called to paint in Hungary, the work was continued by Masaccio who gave us his masterpiece with the « Payment of the Tribute ». As Masaccio left unfinished his cycle of frescos, his work was completed by Filippino Lippi who tried not be less great than his predecessor, but without a doubt, he remained in a field of narrative grace and of documentation with numerous potraits of personages his contemporaries who were found in the frescos.
The frescos, beginning from above the left side represent: 1) *Adam and Eve Kicked out of the Garden of Eden* by Masaccio; 2) *The Payment of the Tribute* by Masaccio; 3) The Preaching of Saint Peter by Masolino; at the right side of the altar; 4) *Saint Peter Baptizing the Neophites* by Masaccio; 5) the left part of the fresco with *Saint Peter Healing the Crippled* is by Masaccio; while the right portion 6) with *Saint Peter Resuscitating Tabita* is by Masomino; 7) *Temptation of Adam,* by Masolino. Below form the left side: 8) *Saint Paul pays a visit to Saint Peter in Prison,* by Filippino Lippi; 8) The left portion of the fresco depicts *Saint Peter Resuscitating the Nephew of the Emperor,* begun by Masaccio and completed by Filippino Lippi: the right portion with *Saint Peter in a Professorial Chair* is by Masaccio; 11) *Saint Peter Healing the Sick with His Own Shade* by Masaccio; 12) *Saint Peter and John Ask for Alms* by Masaccio; 13) *Condemnation and Crucifixion of Saint Peter,* by Filippino Lippi; 14) *The Angel Liberates Saint Peter from Prison,* by Filippino Lippi. In the vault of the chapel is a fresco with the *Madonna Who Gives the Scapular to Beato Simone Stock* by Vincenzo Meucci (1765). - Of interest is also the SACRESTY which we can enter from the left of the Brancacci chapel. Here are found

CHURCH OF SANTA MARIA DEL CARMINE. - **Masaccio:** Detail of the Tribute Money.

CHURCH OF SANTA MARIA DEL CARMINE. — On the left, **Masaccio:** « Adam and Eve expelled from Eden »; on the right, **Masolino:** « Adam and Eve in the Garden of Eden ».

various works of the XIV-XV century among which a polyptych with a *Madonna with Her Child and Saints*, by a follower of Andrea da Firenze and a Crucifix, by a follower of Cimabue. At the extremity of the left arm of the cross-vault is the CORSINI CHAPEL in Baroque style by Pier Francesco Silvani (1675-85). The frescos in the dome are by Luca Giordano. - In the seventeenth century cloister, which we enter from the Sacresty, is a fresco of the XIV cent. with the *Madonna with Her Child and Saints* in Giovanni da Milano's style and *Friars in the Hermitage*, a fragment of a fresco by Filippo Lippi.

Returning into the square and crossing it in all its lenght, we enter Borgo San Frediano where at the left is the CURCH OF SAN FREDIANO IN CASTELLO, rebuilt in 1689 by Antonio Ferri by whom is also the beautiful dome which, if seen from the Americo Vespucci Road along the Arno, adds a picturesque note to the landscape itself.

FOURTH ITINERARY

PIAZZA DEL DUOMO - VIA DEI CERRETANI - VIA TORNABUONI - STROZZI PALACE - PIAZZA SANTA TRINITA (CHURCH OF SANTA TRINITA; CHURCH OF THE APOSTLES) - SANTA TRINITA BRIDGE - LUNGARNO CORSINI (CORSINI GALLERY) - CASCINE PARK - PIAZZA AND CHURCH OF OGNISSANTI - PIAZZA SANTA MARIA NOVELLA (CHURCH AND CLOISTER OF SANTA MARIA NOVELLA).

Via dei Cerretani. — It is one of the city's most animated streets and joins Piazza del Duomo with the Station of Santa Maria Novella. At a certain point on the left this street comes very close to the flank of the CHURCH OF SANTA MARIA MAGGIORE, which has its entrance in the homonymous little square. It is a very ancient church inside the old walls, with traces of Romanesque construction of the X century. The it was rebuilt towards the end of the XIII century. On the portal is a *Madonna and Child*, a sculpture of the Pisan School of the XIV century. The interior, in three ogival naves, contains the *Tomb of Brunetto Latini*, the maestro of Dante. In the chapel at the left of the Presbytery is an *Enthroned Madonna and Child* a painting in relief of the thirteenth century and attributed to Coppo di Marcovaldo. - Continuing along Via dei Cerretani, we reach in a short while the corner in which is located the C.I.T. agency and. turning to the left, we enter Via Rondinelli which leads into Antinori Square.

Piazza Antinori. — It takes its name from the fifteenth century ANTINORI *PALACE* which rises on the right: the construction is attributed to Giuliano da Maiano. Almost opposite the palace rises the CHURCH OF SAN GAETANO of the Romanesque period, but entirely rebuilt in 1648 in Florentine Baroque by Matteo Nigetti, Gherardo and Pier Francesco Silvani. The interior has only one nave and is coverd with black marble. In the second chapel at the left is the *Martyrdom of San Lorenzo* by Pietro da Cortona.

Via Tornabuoni.— It is one of the most aristocratic street in Florence and one of the most beautiful in the world. It is flanked by very beautiful, ancient buildings, shops of art objects, book shops, etc.. On the right, at N.o 19 rises the LARDAREL PALACE, a beautiful construction of late Renaissance architecture erected by Giovanni Antonio Dosio (1580); on the left, at No. 20 is the CORSI PALACE modified in 1875: the original construction was by Michelozzo and by this artist has remained the elegant internal courtyard; at No. 15, the VIVIANI PALACE, (formerly Della Robbia Palace) was the residence of this famous family of artists and was retouched by G. B. Foggini.
At this point we see roads leading to all directions. At the left is Strozzi Street, a beautiful and animated artery which leads to Piazza della Repubblica. At the right are two roads: Via della Spada and Via della Vigna Nuova.

The Palazzo Strozzi and the Palazzo Antinori.

The latter leads to Piazza Rucellai where on the left rises the Loggia Rucellai which was designed by Leon Battista Alberti and built in 1468. Formerly it constituted the favorite place for happy and sad celebrations of the homonymous Florentine family. In the XVII century the admirable work of art was changed into a shop and flat and has remained in this way intil 1963. The Azienda Autonoma del Turismo of Florence has promoted its restoration in order to create a buereau of information for foreign visitors. The project of restoration and adaptation as we actually see it is due to Prof. Piero Sampaolesi from the Institute for the Restoration of Monuments. On the right, at No. 18 of Via della Vigna Nuova, rises the beautiful RUCELLAI PALACE, a masterpiece of architecture of the first par of the Renaissance, erected by Bernardo Rossellino after a design by Leon Battista Alberti (1446-51), which differs from other palaces of the fifteenth century in Florence. It is composed of three floors with the facade in smooth ashlar, separated by beautiful cornices and pilaster strips with ample mullioned windows of traditional character. The valuable courtyard, later retouched, is probably the work of Rossellino. On request, the guard of the palace will be the guide for those interested in visiting the restored RUCELLAI CHAPEL which is found in the near Via della Spada. The chapel contains the *Shrine of the Holy Sepulchre,* a rectangular little temple of Polychromed marbles, the work of Leon Battista Alberti upon invitation of Giovanni di Paolo Rucellai.

Going again along Via della Vigna Nuova in the opposite direction, we return to Via Tornabuoni in the spot where rises the majestic Strozzi Palace.

STROZZI PALACE

It is one of the most beautiful examples of Florentine palaces of the Renaissance. It was begun by Benedetto da Maiano in 1489 after invitation by Filippo Strozzi,

Santa Trinita Bridge. ▶

the rich merchant sent to exile by the hostile Medici. It was during this absence that he got rich. It was later continued by Simone del Pollaiuolo called Cronaca who worked at it from 1497 to 1507, but left it unfinished. In elegant ashlar forms it has two orders of mullioned windows and a magnificent heavy cornice. The angular iron lanterns and the bars that decorated the facades are by Nicolò Grosso called « Caparra » on account of his capricious and bizarre character: he would not carry out any work, whether it were a prince or a citizen to request it, unless a down payment was made. The superb porch courtyard with two orders of loggias, at the interior, is the work of Cronaca.

Continuing along Via Tornabuoni at the left rises the ALTOVITI PALACE with its superior loggia. This palace was joined with the SANGALLETTI PALACE by the architect Silvestri in 1827; at the right at No. 25, is the GIACONI PALACE by Gherardo Silvani (XVII) and at No. 3 the MINERBETTI PALACE of the XIV century. At this point Via Tornabuoni continues after Santa Trinita Square. At the left, cornering with the square, rises the SPINI-FERONI PALACE, an austere construction of the XIII century which preserves the character of a fortress. Opposite, rises the elegant GIANFIGLIAZZI PALACE also of the XII century. After this short walk, flanked by elegant shop windows, the street leads to the avenues along the Arno river and to the Santa Trinita Bridge.

Piazza Santa Trinita. — It rises at the centre of the granite Roman column originating from the Terme di Caracalla (Baths of Caracalla), donated by Pius IV to Cosimo I (1650), surmounted by the porphyry statue depicting *Justice* by Francesco Ferrucci the Younger called Tadda (1581). On the left, at No. 2 rises the BUONDELMONTI PALACE, which belonged to the family which gave bait to the fights between Guelfs and Ghibellines. At N.o 1 rises the BARTOLINI-SALIMBENI PALACE with the facade in clear stone and two orders of windows and niches, the work of Baccio d'Agnolo (1520-29) who caused many polemics on account of the new architectural motif which he created. The architect put on the architrave the Latin inscription « carpere promptius quam imitari » which means that it is easier to criticize than to imitate. From the other side of the square we see the facade of the Church of Santa Trinita.

From the corner of the square begins Borgo SS. Apostoli, one of the most characteristic Medieval roads in Florence, flanked by houses and towers of the XIII-XIV centuries. In this road rises, in a little square, the CHURCH OF THE APOSTLES of the end of the XI century and successively restored. The beautiful portal of the Romanesque facade is of the XVI century and is attributed to Benedetto da Rovezzano. The interior has three naves divided by columns and preserves its original structure. On the door of the sacresty, at the right side of the Presbytery, is the *Sepulchre of Bindo Altoviti* and above the *Statue of Charity*, attributed to Ammannati; left of the high altar is a tabernacle in glazed earthenware by Andrea della Robbia and the *Tomb of Oddo Altoviti* by Benedetto da Rovezzano (1507). In this church is preserved the stone with which we light up the sacred fire for Holy Saturday and which, according to the legend, was brought from the Holy Land by Crusader Pazzino de' Pazzi.

Church of Santa Trinita. ▶

CHURCH OF SANTA TRINITA. - **D. Ghirlandaio:** « The Nativity ».

CHURCH OF SANTA TRINITA

Erected by the monks of Vallombrosa in the XI century, it was rebuilt in 1200 by Niccolò Pisano and successively enlarged. The Baroque facade is by Bernardo Buontalenti (1594), while the *Statue of Saint Alex* at the left and the bas-relief on the central portal with the *Trinity* are by Giovanni Caccini.

The interior is divided into three naves of Gothic style and here are found numerous, important works by artists of the XIV-XV centuries. The lateral chapels were added in the XIV century. In the internal facade are visible the remains of the original Romanesque church. Right nave: on the altar of the third chapel is a *Madonna and Child and Saints* by Neri di Bicci. Fourth chapel, decorated by Lorenzo Monace the maestro of Beato Angelico, with *Stories of Mary* at the walls and *Prophets* in the vault; on the altar, is painting with the *Annunciation*. Fifth chapel, a marble altar by Benedetto da Rovezzano. - Right arm of the cross-vault: past the door of the sacresty, in which is found the *Tomb of Onofrio Strozzi* by Pietro di Niccolò Lamberti.
is the second chapel called the SASSETTI CHAPEL completely frescoed by Domenico Ghirlandaio (1483-86). High in the exterior is a fresco with the statue of David above a painted pilaster and, at the right, the *Sibyl Tiburtina Announcing to Augustus the Birth of Christ*. At the interior in the vault are four *Sibyls* and at the walls is *Stories of Saint Francis*. Beginning from the left and from above: 1) *Renunciation of the Earthly Possession;* 2) *Approval of the Rule;* 3) *The Test of the Fire before the Sultan;* below at the left, 4)*Saint Francis receives the Stigmata;* at the right, 5) *Death of the Saint*. At the altar wall: 6) *Invoked after Death, the Saint Resuscitates the Child of Casa Spini* and below, a *Portrait of Buyer Francesco Sassetti and His Wife Nera Corsi*. On the altar is a painting with a marvelous *Adoration of the Shepherds*, also by Ghirlandaio (1495). At the lateral walls are *Tombs of the Sassetti Couple* attributed to Giuliano da Sangallo

CHURCH OF SANTA TRINITA. — Interior.

(1491). - In the following chapel at the right of the Presbytery is a big Crucifix supposedly by San Giovanni Gualberto because, according to the legend, he bowed his head to indicate approval when Giovanni knealed on it after forgiving the killer of his brother. The Crucifix is covered by a painting which remainds us of the legend. - On the altar of the hight altar is a polyptich with *Trinity and Saints* by Mariotto di Nardo (1416). In the vault and in the large lunettes are frescos by Alessio Baldovinetti (1471). - Left Arm of the cross-vault: in the second chapel at the left of the high chapel is a very beautiful *Tomb of the Bishop from Fiesole Benozzo Federighi* a work in marble by Luca della Robbia (1456); at the walls, *Stories of Saint Bartholomew* by Giovanni da Ponte. In the second chapel, *Christ Meets Mary* at the Calvary of the Florentine School of the XV century. - Left nave: in the fifth chapel is a wooden statue of the *Magdalen* by Desiderio da Settignano (1464) and completed by Benedetto da Maiano (1468). In the fourth chapel, on the altar is the *Crowning of the Virgin* of the Senese School of the fifteenth century; marked with a headstone is the *Tomb of Dino Compagni* (1250-1324) the friend of Dante and a chronicler of his time. The third chapel has on the altar a painting by Neri di Bicci with the *Annunciation* and at the walls frescos of the School of Giotto depicting the *Disputation of Santa Caterina;* the Roman sarcophagus with the lying statue is the *Tomb of Giuliano Davanzati*. On the altar of the second chapel is the *Mystic Wedding of Saint Catherine*, by Antonio del Ceraiolo (XVI century); at the walls, *Saint Jerome in Penitence* and the *Annunciation*, frescos by Ridolfo del Ghirlandaio (1503). - On request, the guard will guide the visitor to the Roman crypt which can be reached by means of a staircase in the middle of the central nave. In the crypt are preserved remains of the ancient church.

Santa Trinita Bridge. — It is the most majestic of the bridges on the Arno. The bridge was firs built in 1252 by architects of Santa Maria Novella fathers Sisto and Ristoro. Ruined in 1557, it was rebuilt by Bartolomeo Ammannati in 1567-69 under the influence of Michelangelo, who created one of the most beautiful bridges in Italian architecture during the Renaissance with three arches supported by powerful pillars. The statues depicting the four seasons decorate the entrances; they were added in 1608. Destroyed by the war during the night of August 4, 1944, it has been faithfully rebuilt « as it was and where it was » by Engineer Emilio Brizzi and by the Architect Riccardo Gizdulich (1955-57), using a large portion of the original material.

Lungarno Corsini. (Corsini Avenue along the Arno river) — It is the most beautiful walk along the Arno. The name derives from the Corsini family which had many illustrious members such as Lorenzo Corsini who became Pope Clement XII (XVIII century) and Andrea Corsini, the Bishop of Fiesole. The Lungarno is flanked by noble buildings: At No. 2, which is the British Consulate, rises the Gianfigliazzi Palace which was modified in the XIX century together with the Renaissance building that follows, always by Gianfigliuzzi. At No. 10 is the CORSINI PALACE built by P. F. Silvani and A. Ferri (1648-56), consisting of a central body and two lateral wings with beautiful terraces adorned with statues. It is among the best examples of Florentine Baroque. At the back of the courtyard at the left is a big spiral staircase by Silvani and at the right the monumental one by Ferry with various ancient statues among which that of Clement XII. - At the first floor of the palace is the CORSINI GALLERY founded by Prince Lorenzo Corsini in 1765. It is one of the most conspicuous collections in Italy, rich of valuable paintings by Raffaello, Filippino Lippi, Andrea del Castagno, Botticelli, Signorelli, Caravaggio, Andrea del Sarto and other Italians and foreigners of the XVII-XVIII centuries. Corsini Avenue ends where it meets on the left the rebuilt Carraia Bridge and on the right with Goldoni Square. Continuing instead along the same direction we enter Lungarno Amerigo Vespucci which leads to Ognissanti Square which opens at the right.
Continuing along Lungarno Amerigo Vespucci where we enjoy a beautiful view of the southern side of the city with the characteristic dome of the Cestello Church, we see Mount Oliveto in the background and the Hill of San Miniato on the left; further ahead we find the bridge dedicated to the great navigator Amerigo Vespucci who discovered the coast line of Brasil. It is the most modern bridge in Florence built in 1957 after a project of Architects Enzo Gori, Giuseppe Gori, Ernesto Nelli and Engineer Riccardo Morandi. The lungarno ends where, at the left, is rebuilt the bridge of Victory and, on the right, where we see the spacious and green Square of Vittorio Veneto ornated at the centre by the *Equestrian Statue of Vittorio Emanuele II;* the work of Emilio Zocchi (1890). Here begins the vast CASCINE PARK with long avenues, trees, and big green meadows. This park is over 3 kilometers in length on the right side of the Arno river. Originally this spacious park was the property of the Medicis who used it asa stable and as a pasture ground for animals: for this reason it is called « Cascine ». It was opened to the public about the middle of the XVIII century and from then on it has become one of the favorite walks of the Florentines. In this vast green zone have their headquarters the Agrarian Institute, the Aeronautics Academy and various sport installations among which the hippodrome, the court for ball games, tennis courts, the Bicycle Track. At the end of the rectilinear avenues of the Cascine rises the *Monument to the Indian Majarà of Kolopoor* who died at the age of twenty in Florence in 1870. The

Church of Ognissanti.

Church of Santa Maria Novella.

monument was erected on the spot in which the prince was cremated; namely, at the junction of two rivers (the Mugnone with the Arno) according to the rite of Bramante. This locality is called by the Florentines « the Indian ». The Cascine Park is where each year is celebrated the traditional and popular « grasshopper feast ».

Piazza Ognissanti. — Flanked by big hotels, it has at the centre the modern group of sculptures representing *Hercules Killing the Lion,* the work of Romanelli. As a background to the square we have the Baroque facade of the OGNISSANTI CHURCH, erected in the XII century and rebuilt in the XVII century. In the lunette above the portal is a glazed earthenware with the *Crowing of the Virgin* by Benedetto Buglioni. The trim bell tower is of the primitive thirteenth century construction. The interior, with only one nave with a transept, preserves valuable works of art. At the second altar at the right is a fresco by Domenico Ghirlandaio depicting the *Vespucci Family under the Cloak of the Madonna* (1470); among the various personages, the young man dressed in red between the Madonna and the Old Man, is Amerigo. Between the third and the fourth altar is a very beautiful fresco by Botticelli depicting *Saint Augustine in his Studio* (1480). In the chapel of the right arm is a little disc indacating the place in which rest the mortal remains of Botticelli. The frescos in the dome and in the architectural brackets of the major chapel are by Giovanni da San Giovanni (1617). Between the third and the fourth altar of the left wall, opposite the one in front is the fresco with *Saint Jerome in His Studio,* the work of Domenico Ghirlandaio (1480). - From the window of the church we enter the Renaissance cloister with lunettes frescoed by Giovanni da San Giovanni (1616-19) and Iacopo Ligozzi (1625) with the *Stories of Saint Francis.* A door of the cloister leads into the famous *Supper* the masterpiece of Domenico Ghirlandaio (1480). It is said that Leonardo da Vinci was inspired by this composition to make his famous « Supper » which is found the the ex convent of the Dominican Fathers at the Church of Santa Maria delle Grazie in Milano.

Going along the Borgognissanti road we reach Via dei Fossi which leads into the vast square of Santa Maria Novella.

Piazza Santa Maria Novella. — It is one of the most beautiful and imposing squares in Florence, dominated by the marble facade of the church that gives it its name. On the opposite side of the church rises the beautiful fifteenth century LOGGIA OF SAINT PAUL with arcades on columns and decorated with medallions in terracotta by Giovanni della Robbia; under the perch, is a beautiful lunette by Andrea della Robbia with the *Meeting of Saint Dominic and Francis.* The two marble obelisks at the middle of the square, surmounted by a bronze lilly and resting on bronze tortoises, are by Giambologna (1608): they marked the limits of the square for the famous charriot races of Roman inspiration and instituted by Cosimo I in 1563.

CHURCH OF SANTA MARIA NOVELLA

A church of the Dominican order, it is one of the most famous in Florence. A masterpiece of Gothic architecture it was built by two friars of the order, Sisto da Firenze and Ristoro da Campi who began it in 1279. It was finished in 1360 by another friar Iacopo Talenti who was the builder of the agile Gothic-roman bell tower also. The building, a typical example of Gothic-florentine architecture, with the decorations of the facade in green and white marble, was completed between 1456 and 1470 by Leon Battista Alberti who added the upper portion of the facade and the central portal which has a Renaissance character, so that from the wedding of styles is born a new source of harmony. At the sides of the facade and on the external wall of the cloisters are the tombs, in Gothic style, belonging to famous Florentine families.

THE INTERIOR, of harmonious and slim Gothic architecture, is in the shape of an Egyptian cross with three naves joined by pillars and vaulted arches. The altars of the minor naves are by Giorgio Vasari (1565-71). Right nave: in the second span is a Monument of *Beata Villana dei Cerchi* by Bernardo Rossellino (1451). After the fifth span we have access to the PURA CHAPEL of 1474 with a wooden cross on the high altar painted with *Stories of Jesus,* of the beginning of the XIV century. The door at the right leads inside the ancient cemetery with tombal niches and coats-of-arms. Right arm of the transept: at the right, a tabernacle with *Bust of Saint Anthony in Terracotta* of the XV century; high in the wall is a *Gothic Tomb of Bishop Tedice Aliotti* of Fiesole (d. 1336), the work of the Senese Tino di Camaino; above at the left is the *Tomb of Aldobrando Cavalcanti the Bishop of Orvieto* by Nino Pisano; below, is the Tomb of *Giuseppe the Patriarch of Constantinople* who died in Florence in 1439. From the butt-end of the transept we go up to the RUCELLAI CHAPEL where is located the famous Madonna by Duccio di Boninsegna, now at the Uffizi Gallery, and painted around the year 1285. At the walls are remains of frescos of the XIV century depicting the *Martyrdom of Saint Catherine*. At the wall back of the transept is the BARDI CHAPEL, or the Sacramento Chapel, with remains of frescos of the School of Giotto; at the right pillar of the entrance is *Saint George Giving Blessings*, a relief of the XIII century; at the right, is a mullioned window of the thirteenth century, a remaining part of the primitive construction. Then follows the FILIPPO·STROZZI CHAPEL with frescos by Filippino Lippi (1503) depicting *Stories of Apostles Filippo and Giovanni*, one of the last works of the artist; in the vault, is *Adam, Noah, Abraham and Jacob*. Behind the altar is a beautiful *tomb of Filippo Strozzi* by Benedetto da Maiano. CHAPEL OF THE HIGH ALTAR: before the steps is a bronze *tcmbal slab of Leonardo Dati*, by Lorenzo Ghiberti (1423) and at the right of the altar, is a very beautiful chandelier by Pier Giovanni Tedesco (XIV century): at the left, is an imitation of the same. On the modern altar is a *Crucifix in bronze* by Giambologna. - Apse: the wooden choir and the reading desk are by Baccio d'Agnolo and retouched by Vasari. In the vault and on the walls is the famous cycle of frescos, the masterpiece of Ghirlandaio and his helper among whom Michelangelo as a young man (1485-90), with *Stories of Mary and of the Baptist*. In these frescos are portraits of personages of the Tornabuoni family, and friends with costumes of the time, so that these paintings assume the value of a Florentine chronicle and of a history of costumes. In the vault is the *Evangelists* and, in the left wall, *Stories of Mary*, which beginning from the left at the bottom depict: 1) *Gioacchino kicked out of the Temple for not Having an Offspring;* 2) *Birth of the Virgin;* 3) *Presentation to the Temple;* 4) the *Wedding of the Virgin;* 5) *Adoration of the Magi;* 6) *Massacre of the Innocents;* in the lunett, *Death and Assumption of the Virgin*. Back wall: in the lunette is the *Crowning of the Virgin;* at the sides of the large window, *Saint Dominic burns Heretical Books; Death of Saint Peter the Martyr; Annunciation; San Giovannino goes to the Desert*. Below, in the golden figures are the portraits of Francesco Tornabuoni and his wife Francesca Pitti, the buyers of the frescos. At the right wall is *Stories of Saint John the Baptist*: from below to the right, *Apparition of the Angel to Zachariah; Visitation; Birth of the Baptist; Saint Zachariah writes the Name of Giovanni; Preaching of the Baptist; Baptism of Jesus;* in the lunette, is the *Banquet of Herod*. Left transept: GONDI CHAPEL, with remains of thirteenth century frescos by Greek painters and a wooden *Crucifix* by Filippo Brunelleschi, also called « Christ of the eggs » because Donatello who had made a Crucifix which was criticized by Brunelleschi (now in the church of Santa Croce), seeing it was so beautifully made, dropped the eggs he had in his lap for the wonder. Then follows the GADDI CHAPEL with stuccos and paintings in the vault by Alessandro Allori and on the altar, a painting by Agnolo Bronzino with the *Miracle of Jesus*. We go on to the left arm of the transept and we enter, preceded by a staircase, the STROZZI CHAPEL, with frescos by Nardo di Cione (1357) depicting the *Universal Judgement*, on the back wall; *Paradise*, on the left wall and *Hell* in the one at the right, inspired according to the conception of Dante. In Paradise we note the portrait of Dante dead a few years before the making of the frescos. On the altar, a beautiful painting

The Carraia Bridge and the suggestive dome of the church of Cestello.

by Andrea Orcagna with *Triumphant Jesus* (1357). From the left wall of the transept we enter the SACRESTY architected by Iacopo Talenti (1350), in which particularly notable are: a washstand in terracotta by Giovanni della Robbia (1498); a Crucifix attributed to Giotto and another attributed to Maso di Bartolomeo.

Left nave: marvelous is the big fresco at the hall depicting the *Holy Trinity* by Masaccio (1428). It is one of the last works by the maestro containing an emphasized and airy perspective and of a great humanity. The pillar next to the last is the pulpit, made after a design by Brunelleschi by his pupil Andrea Cavalcanti called Buggiano (1462). Right of the first altar is a *Tomb of Lawyer A. Strozzi* by Andrea Ferrucci from Fiesole and helpers (1524).

Cloister of Santa Maria Novella. — The entrance is left of the facade of the church. The first we come across is the GREEN CLOISTER, which is also the most ancient cloister built about 1350 by Father Giovanni da Campi and inspired to the Romanesque style. It is so called on account of the colour of the frescos in green earth, made by Paolo Uccello in the XIV century. The fragments which have remained in the cloister are probably by his pupils, while the two preserved in a room of the refectory depicting *Scenes of the Universal Floor* and *Stories of Noah,* are by the maestro. In the cloister is found the *Big Chapel of the Spaniards* so called because Eleonora di Toledo, the wife of Cosimo I de' Medici, assigned it to the gentlemen of her following. It was the ancient capitular hall of the order built by Iacopo Talenti in 1359 in honour of San Tommaso d'Aquino and decorated with frescos by Andrea di Bonaiuto called Andrea da Firenze (1366-68), a Florentine painter who felt the influence of the Gothic-senese style. The paintings, on subjects dictated by the theologian of the order Father Zenobi of Guasconi the Prior of the convent, represent: in the left wall, the *Triumph of Saint Thomas Aquinas;* in the right wall, the *Militant Church;* in the back wall and in the vault, *Scenes of the New Testament.* The whole is rich of symbols and of theological doctrine to constitute a real treatise. In the entrance wall are *Stories of Saint Peter the Martyr.* - Left of the Big Chapel of the Spaniards, through a corridor, we enter the LITTLE CLOISTER OF THE DECEASED, in which are sepulchral tombs of the Strozzis decorated with frescos of the School of Orcagna. The lunette with « Noli me tangere », is from the workshop of the Della Robbias. - From here we can have access into the BIG CLOISTER, one of the most imposing in Florence with 50 arcades and frescos of the XVI-XVII centuries: actually it is occupied by the young officers' school for Carabinieri.

CENACULUM OF SANT'APOLLONIA. - **A. del Castagno:** Farinata degli Uberti.

DOMINVS FARINATA DEVBERTIS SVE PATRIE LIBERATOR

FIFTH ITINERARY

PIAZZA DEL DUOMO - VIA CAVOUR - CENACOLO DI SANT'APOLLONIA - CLOISTER OF SCALZO - PIAZZA SAN MARCO (CHURCH OF SAN MARCO; MUSEUM OF SAN MARCO OR OF ANGELICO) - GALLERY OF THE ACADEMY - PIAZZA SS. ANNUNZIATA (CHURCH OF SS. ANNUNZIATA; SPEDALE DEGLI INNOCENTI; ARCHAEOLOGICAL MUSEUM) - SYNAGOGUE - CONVENT OF SANTA MARIA MADDALENA DE' PAZZI - CHURCH OF SAINT AMBROSE.

Via Cavour. — It is the continuation of Martelli Street which starts from Piazza del Duomo. It is one of the main and most animated arteries in the city, flanked by severe palaces of the XVII - XVIII centuries which give it a noble appearance. At the beginning of the left corner rises the Medici-Riccardi Palace which we have described in the first itinerary. In the point where Cavour Street crosses laterally San Marco Square, on the left is Arazzieri Street which at the end leads into Via XVII Aprile where at No. 1 is the monastery of Saint Apollonia. Further on, at No. 63 of Cavour Street rises the imposing palace where has its headquarters the Court of Appeals, which occupies the zone which was the MEDICI CLUB OF SAN MARCO constituted by a marvelous garden bought in the fifteenth century by Claire Orsini, the wife of Lorenzo il Magnifico. It was for merit of these people that developed the artistic and cultural life of Florence at that time. Here, as a matter of fact, gathered artists, men of letters and all those ingenious people that were part of the court of Lorenzo; here he gathered ancient statues, Roman bas-reliefs and works by contemporaries. - Further ahead, at No. 69 is the cloister of Scalzo.

Cenacolo di Sant'Apollonia. (Supper Room of Saint Apollonia) - (The entrance is at Via XVII Aprile No. 1. To visit, please advise the guard). It is the ancient refectory of the Benedictine convent of Saint Apollonia, where are preserved the frescos by Andrea del Castagno (1450-57). One of the most meaningful works by the artist is here represented with the famous *Last Supper* of an intense realism. At the walls of the same artist is the cycle of frescos originating from Villa Pandolfini di Legnaia, depicting great personages of history and poetry, conceived in a perspective-architectural environment: *Boccaccio, Petrarch, Dante, Queen Tamiris, Queen Esther, Sibyl Cumana, Niccolò Acciaiuoli, Farinata degli Uberti and Pippo Spano.* At the left wall is the *Crucifion, Deposition and Resurrection.* In the two lunettes, *Crucifixion and Saints* and the *Pietà.*

Cloister of Scalzo. — (Cavour Street N.º 69. To visit, it is necessary to advise the guard). It is so called because the carrier of the Cross of the religious fraternity founded in 1376, used to walk in processions bare-footed. It is a small courtyard, rectangular in shape and with porticos of the beginning of the XVI century, with the walls frescoed in chiaroscuro by Andrea del Sarto depicting sixteen episodes of the life of Saint John the Baptist. They were begun by the artist in 1514 and finished in 1526. Two episodes are by Franciabigio.

Piazza San Marco. — It is a vast square ornamented with gardens with the *Monument to General Manfredo Fanti* at the centre by Pio Fedi (1837). It is surrounded by the Church of San Marco with the convent where is the Saint Mark Museum (or the Museum of the Angelico). Here are also the Administrative centre of the UNIVERSITY OF FLORENCE and the Faculty of Letters. Cornering with Via Ricasoli is the fourteenth century porch of the ACADEMY OF FINE ARTS, which was part of the Hospital of Saint Matthew. Under the porch are a lunette frescoed by Mariotto di Nardo (1413) and three terracottas by the Della Robbias. - At N.° 52 of Via Ricasoli is the headquarters of the Academy and the Tribune of David.

CHURCH OF SAN MARCO

Erected at the end of the XIII century in Romanesque-gothic style, it was almost completely rebuilt in 1452 by Michelozzo and by desire of Cosimo the Elder who destined it to the Dominican fathers. In 1580 it was retouched by Giambologna and, finally, in 1678, it was greatly modified by Pier Francesco Silvani to whom we owe its present appearance. The Baroque facade is by Fra Gioacchino Pronti (1780), while the wooden door is still the one that existed at the time of Savonarola. This door resisted to an attempt on the part of the people to burn it in order to enter the church and capture the friar and make their justice.

THE INTERIOR, with only one nave, has at the centre the engraved painting with the *Madonna in Glory*, by G .Antonio Pucci (1725). Above the entrance door is a great *Crucifix* of the School of Giotto. At the first altar of the right wall is *Saint Thomas Aquinas* by Santi di Tito; at the second *Madonna and Saints* by Father Bartolomeo (1509); at the third, is a great mosaic with the *Virgin in Prayer* of the VIII century and originating from the oratorio of Pope Giovanni VII; at the fourth, (let us notice the arch by Giambologna (1580), is a *Madonna with the Image of Saint Dominic* by Matteo Rosselli. At the summit of the arch is a *Statue of San Zanobi* by Giambologna. In the back, through a Baroque door, we enter the vestibule and in the sacresty architected by Michelozzo (1437-43), in which is found at the left the bronze *Statue of Saint Antonino*, made by Domenico Portigiani after a design by Giambologna. At the left of the Major Chapel is the Serragli or Sacramento Chapel decorated with frescos by Santi di Tito and by Passignano. Then follows the Salviati Chapel or of Saint Antonino, built in 1580-89 after a design by Giambologna in which are found valuable frescos by Passignano depicting the *Transferring of the Saint*. The bronze and marble decorations are by Giambologna and this pupil *Giovanni Pico the Count of Mirandola* and by *Agnolo Ambrogini* called Poliziano.

MUSEUM OF SAINT MARK (or of ANGELICO)

The entrance is located at the right of the church and has its headquarters in the building which was originally the convent of the Vallombrosani Monks and later of the

MUSEUM OF SAINT MARK. - **Beato Angelico:**
« The Flight into Egypt ».

MUSEUM OF SAINT MARK. - **Beato Angelico:** « Crucifixion ».

MUSEUM OF SAINT MARK. - **Beato Angelico:**
« Madonna » and « Coronation of the Virgin ».

Silvestrinis. By will of Cosimo the Elder it was entirely rebuilt by Michelozzo (1437-57) when the convent had already been destined to the Dominican fathers of Fiesole where also was Father Giovanni called Beato Angelico who lived there from 1435-1445. Later lived here Girolamo Savonarola, from 1498; Saint Antonino Pierozzi, the Archbishop of Florence; Father Bartholomew, the

MUSEUM OF SAINT MARK. - **Beato Angelico:**
« Deposition from the Cross ».

great Renaissance painter. When the acurties of the Convent were interrupted in 1866, it became a State Museum where were kept for the most part the works of Beato Angelico which were at that time scattered in the severall galleries and churches of Florence, thus forming a museum of exceptional interest.

CLOISTER OF SAINT ANTONINO. - Of monastic architecture of the Renaissance, it has under the porch frescos of the XVI-XVII centuries which narrate episodes of the life of Saint Antonino. Interesting is the fresco by Bernardino Poccetti in the lunette near the entrance of the hostel which depicts the facade by Arnolfo of the Cathedral of Florence. By Beato Angelico are: in the back and at the left in the little lunette above the door *Saint Peter the Martyr*; at the wall before the entrance *Saint Dominic at the Feet of the Crucifix*; in the back of the same wall in the lunette above the door is the *Pietà*; on the door of the following wall is *Jesus Dressed as a Pilgrim Received by the Dominican Fathers*.

HÓSTEL OF PILGRIM. - It contains paintings by Angelico. All the works by this artist aim at glorifying faith, adoring and exalting Divine Love. This place is divided into three sections separated by parapets. In the first section at the left is the large Linaioli Tabernacle with the *Enthroned Virgin and Musician Angels* (1433), with the beautiful marble cornice made after a design by Ghiberti. Interesting, in this first section, are also the *Wedding and Death of the Virgin*; *Saint Zachariah Writing His Son's Name*; two *Enthroned* Madonna; the *Miracle* and the *Burial of Cosma and Damiano*. In the second section are exposed 35 little pictures with Stories of Christ which used to form (1450) the windows of the Tabernacle of Crucifixion in the Church of SS. Annunziata. Those depicting the *Flight to Egypt*, the *Nativity* and the *Entrance of Jesus into Gerusalem* are by Angelico; the others were made in collaboration with others and three are by Alessio Baldovinetti. In the third section are very beautiful paintings such as the *Madonna of the Star*; the *Final Judgement*; the *Crowning of the Virgin*; *Deposition from the Cross*; *Annunciation*: *Epiphany*.

THE WASHSTAND ROOM. - Here is the Paptismal font, of the workshop of the Della Robbias. At the walls are paintings of the XVI century among which a large *Madonna and Saints* in chiaroscuro by Father Bartolomeo.

GREAT REFECTOR. - The hall with a cross vault has at the walls works by Father Bartholomew, among which the *Final Judgement*. The large fresco at the back wall with the *Miraculous Supper of Saint Dominic* is by Giovanni Antonio Sogliani (1536).

CAPITOLAR ROOM. - It is where the friars, after confessing their sins, waited for punishment from their superior. As a matter of fact, *Saint Thomas Aquinas Presenting the Book of Discipline* in the lunette above the door, symbolizes the function of the place. At the wall before the entrance is the dramatic and seraphic composition of the *Crucifixion with the Madonna, Maries, Saints and Founders of the Religious Orders*, a stupendous work by Angelico.

At the left wall is *Saint Antonino in Prayer*, a painting in destemper by Alessio Baldovinetti. At the right wall is a Crucifix in polychromed wood by Baccio da Montelupo (1500).

FIRST FLOOR. - After going up the steep staircase which leads to the upper floor, opposite we see the wonderful fresco of a profound mysticism depicting *Annunciation* and at the left the *Crucifix Adored by Saint Dominic*, stupendous works by Angelico.

GALLERY OF THE ACCADEMIA. - **Michelangelo:** Saint Matthew. ▶

At the sides of the corridors are the small cells with barrel vaults which were at one time the dwelling of the Dominican Fathers.

Each has a fresco by Angelico or of one of his pupils who made it after a design of the maestro. The most notable frescos, made by Angelico, are: cell 1, « Noli me tanger »; cell 3, *Annunciation;* cell 4. *Crucifixion;* cell 6, *Transfiguration,* cell 7, *Christ Derided;* cell 9, *Crowning of Mary;* cell 11, *Madonna with Child and Saints.* Back of the corridor is the QUARTERS OF THE PRIOR made up of three cells in which lived Girolamo Savonarola, the famous Reformer who was burned. It was in this very convent that on April 8, 1498 he was taken for the execution of the death sentence. In the first cell (vestibule), are two paintings of the period depicting the execution of Savonarola (23 of May 1498); *Portrait of Savonarola* and *Portrait of Saint Peter the Martyr,* both by Father Bartolomeo. In the second cell (studio), is a wooden *Crucifix* by Baccio da Montelupo, bèlonging to Savonarola. On the writing desk are two bibles and in a little cupboard of the sixteenth century, at the wall, two calices, a cloak, the tunic and the crown: objects belonging to the friar. In the other cell (bedroom of Savonarola) is a coat-of-arms with the *Crucifix,* in the manner of Angelico. Coming back we visit the cells of the left wall frescoed with Crucifixes made by Angelico's helpers. In cell 31, which was Saint Antonino's, are preserved codes handritten by the Saint, a few relics and the funeral mask of the Bishop. In the entrance corridor, in cell 34, is *Prayer in the Orchard,* and in cell 35, *Comunion of the Apostles,* notable frescos made by helpers of Beato Angelico. Back of the corridor at the right, cells 38 and 39 were reserved to Cosimo the Elder when he retired in meditation in the convent. In the first cell *Jesus Crucified and Saints,* a painting by Angelico with the collaboration of Benozzo Gozzoli. In the second is a *Bust in Terracotta of Saint Antonino* and *Cosimo's Portrait* attributed to Pontormo.

LIBRARY. - Returning to the main floor, at the right we enter the refectory decorated with a large fresco by Domenico Ghirlandaio depicting the *Last Supper,* a replica with some variation of the Cenacolo (Supper room) by Ognissanti.

CLOISTER OF SAINT DOMINIC. - Architected by Michelozzo, along the porches and in the adjacent places, it contains architectural fragments of the ancient Medieval centre of Florence, demolished towards the end of the XIX century. In the centre of the cloister, rises the *Statue of Saint Dominic* by Andrea Baratta (1700).

GALLERY OF THE ACADEMY

It is necessary to note that the gallery, actually, is being reordered in the section of paintings. The location of the works is therefore likely to undergo displacement after completion of the restoration. At any event the numbering of the halls are going to be the same as will be found in this book. The gallery consists of nine halls in addition to the spacious room containging the masterpieces of Michelangelo.

This gallery can be considered to be founded by Grandduke Pietro Leopoldo I of Lorena in 1784, who wanted to give to the young people attending the Accademy of Fine Arts an opportunity to study the past by putting at their disposal a nucleus of paintings which, as time went by, has become richer and richer with works originating from churches and convents. The collections has under-

GALLERY OF THE ACADEMY. — **Michelangelo:** « David ».

gone changes due especially to new critiria of arrangement of Florentine museums. At present here are located minor works by famous painters, but, not less important, those who flourished between 1200 and 1500. The gallery, however, owes its fame to the presence of the sculpture masterpieces of the great maestro Michelan-

GALLERY OF THE ACCADEMIA. - **Michelangelo: Slaves.**

gelo Buonarroti. As a matter of fact in this place the architect Emilio De Fabris thought of and built the « shining » tribune to give hospitality to the famous statues of David which was at one time located in front of the Palazzo Vecchio in Piazza della Signoria and here transferred to save it from the dangers of storms. The David was taken here in 1873 and located in the tribune in 1882.

Past the entrance hall we can enter the great nave which has the statue of David in the background. We need not have a special competence to understand that we are here before the power of the superhuman genius of Michelangelo which manifests itself immediately with the presence of the very famous « Prisons » four roughly sketched sculptures which, together with the others preserved in the museum of Louvre in Paris, were destined to the tomb of Pontiff Giulius II in Rome (1518) planned by the artist but never completed by him. Further on is the *Statue of Saint Matthew,* unfinished (1505), the only one of the figure of twelve Apostles which Michelangelo had carried out and which were to be made for the cathedral of Florence. It we observe well these sculptures, we discover that their beauty consists in the very fact that they were never completed. The conception of Michelangelo gives us a synthesis of his power of plastic expression; the artist has aggressively worked the piece of marble so as to to create a figure with a feverishly expressive character, tormented by the desire of freeing from the material a live form. Michelangelo did not complete many of his works, perhaps because the sole sketch had already satisfied his creative thirst. It we look at these « Prigioni », we note how they are no longer matter, but an expression of sorrow and strength in the vane and desperate attempt to get away from the immobility to which the artists had condemned them. Behind the sculptures, at the walls, are Flemish and Florentine arrasses of the XVI-XVII-XVIII centuries representing the various episodes of the Genesis. Right after the Saint Matthew we see the very famous *Pietà di Palestrina* which is in the gallery from 1939 and which Buonarrotti sculptured at a late period for the chapel of the Barberini palace in Palestrina. This work has been much discussed by critics because of its attribution to Michelangelo; the fact that it was not finished and the very apparent reality of the sensation of pain and death make us certain that the attribution is correct. In the tribune stands imposing the famous *David* commissioned to Michelangelo by the Florentine Republic in order to have a symbol of liberty before the Comune (City Hall) where it has been now substituted with a copy. It is the artist's early work: begun at the age of 26, it was completed four years later (1501-4). This gigantic figure is indeed very beautiful in its aspect of pride and virility, physical prowess and nobility of expressions which show us with how much adherence to symbol this had been conceived by Buonarroti. However, keeping in mind that the masterpiece has come out of the hands of a young man with a very precocious talent, the work is not to be considered perfect at least as far as anatomical proportions are concerned. As a matter of fact its sides are thin in contrast with a rather well developed back, the same can be said of the head, the hands and feet result slightly bigger than it would be necessary; but these are defects which are canceled by the colossal impostation of the whole nude protracted as it is towards the objective of facing with calm and firmness the ferocity of the opponent. From the left of the tribune of David, we enter the halls of exposition.

Let us note first, however, the *Bust of Michelangelo* made by Daniele da Volterra, and always from this side the painting with the *Crowning of the Virgin Among Musician Angels and Saints,* by Spinello Aretino, Niccolò Gerini, Lorenzo di Niccolò (provisional location); at the left is the *Annunciation and Saints,* by Giovanni del Biondo and the *Crowning of the Virgin,* by Rossello di Iacopo Franchi (these two also of provisional location). In a visit to the halls, we shall point out the major works.

Room I. - The Crucifix, of the Senese school of the second half of the XIII century; the *Crucifixion with Madonna and Saints,* by Pacino di Buonaguida (1310); under the glass; is the *Virgin among Archaengels Gabriel and Michael with sixteen Saints*, from the Cretese Venetian School of the XV century; the *Tree of the Cross*, by Pacino di Buonaguida.

ROOM II. - At the back wall is a great *Crucifix*, of the Florentine school of the beginning of the XV century; under the glass, are *Episodes of the Life of Saints*, by Agnolo Gaddi; *Trinity*, by Nardo di Cione; Madonna and Four Saintes, by Andrea di Cione called Orcagna; the *Crowning of the Virgin*, a tryptich by Bernardo Gaddi.

ROOM III. - The *Crucifix*, from the school of Bernardo Daddi of the middle of the XV century; under the glass, a *Madonna and Saints with Crucifixion, and Saints*, by the so called maestro of the Childhood of Christ; *Madonna and Child*, by Taddeo Gaddi the cornice of whom is by Niccolò di Pietro Gerini; *14 Stories of the life of Christ* and *Ten Scenes of the Life of Saint Francis*, attributed to Taddeo Gaddi and which were part of the relies closed in the sacresty of Santa Croce.

ROOM IV. - It is an imposing hall which was previously divided into two portions. Here have been opened large windows in the walls so that it would become very brilliant. At present it is closed for restoration, but as soon as it will be ready it will contain works by Neri di Bicci, by Lorenzo Monaco and other great artists whose works are presently located in various halls or in a provisional storage place.

To reach the V hall it is necessary to return to the nave of the David and to enter the door which opens between the Pietà di Palestrina and the statue of Saint Matthew.

ROOM V. - Here is located the front part of a big trunk of the fifteenth century which represents the Nuptial Feast in Piazza San Giovanni of the *Boccacci-Adimari-Ricasoli Wedding*, representing a vivacious picture of Florentine customs of the period; *Episodes of the Virgin's Life and Her Glorification*, by Mariotto Cristofano (1393-1457); *San Bernardino and Tobiolo with Angels* by Domenico di Michelino; *Madonna in Throne and Saints* by Cosimo Rosselli; *Annunciation*, by Filippino Lippi.

ROOM VI. - *Madonna of the Sea* and *Virgin with Angels*, two works by Sandro Botticelli; *Meeting of the Virgin with Saint Elizabeth*, by Pietro Perugino; *Tebaide*, by Paolo Uccello; *SS. Trinità*, by Alessio Baldovinetti designed in 1471; *Pietà* by Sebastiano Mainardi.

ROOM VII. - *Adoration of the Child*, by Cosimo Rosselli; *Nativity*, by Lorenzo di Credi (1459-1537); *Madonna in Throne with Child and Saints* by Botticelli; *Resurrection* by Raffaellino del Garbo; *Deposition* by Iacopo del Sellaio (1441-93).

ROOM VIII. - *Assumption and Saints* by Francesco Granacci; *Assumption*, by Perugino (1500); *Deposition*, by Perugino and Filippino Lippi; *Apparition of the Virgin to Saint Bernard*, by Fra Bartolomeo della Porta (1507); *Removal of the Corpse of San Zanobi* and *San Zanobi Resuscitates a Child*, by two works by Ridolfo del Ghirlandaio (1483-1561); *Trinity*, by Mariotto Albertinelli; *Madonna della Cintola*, by Francesco Granacci; *Saint Jerome*, by Bartolomeo di Giovanni of the second hall of the XV century; *Madonna in the Well*, already attributed to Raffaello, by Franciabigio the Florentine (1482-1525); in the middle of the hall are *squares with stories of Saints*, by Francesco Granacci.

ROOM IX. - *Deposition*, by Bronzino; *Annunciation*, by Alessandro Allori; *Murder of the Innocents*, by Daniele Ricciarelli da Volterra; *Charity*, by Francesco Morandini called Poppi; *Venus and Love*, by Iacopo Carucci called Pontormo; *Saint John in the Desert*, by Raffaello; *Entrance of Jesus into Jerusalem*, by Santi di Tito.

From the Academy we return to San Marco Square from where, at the right, Via Cesare Battisti leads to SS. Annunziata Square.

GALLERY OF THE ACCADEMIA. - **Michelangelo:** The Palestrina Pietà. ▶

Piazza SS. Annunziata. — It is the Florentine square which includes in it the harmony of the Renaissance spirit, the perfect equilibrium of dimensions, the serene balance which typified Florentine architecture during the Renaissance. It is surrounded with airy porches and ornated at the centre with the famous *Equestriam statue of Grand·Duke Ferdinand I*, a late work by Giambologna finished by Pietro Tacca (1608). Not far from the monument are two elegant Baroque fountains with figures of marine monsters in bronze, works by Tacca and his helpers (1629). The background is provided by the porch and the facade of the Church of SS. Annunziata and it is limited on the right by the Brunelleschian porch of the Spedale degli Innocenti (the hospital) and on the left the porch of the CONFRATERNITY OF THE SERVANTS OF MARY, erected by Antonio da Sangallo the Elder and Baccio d'Agnolo (1516-25).

Spedale degli Innocenti. — It is among the first Renaissance works in Florence and was made by Filippo Brunelleschi who began it in 1421 and worked at it until 1424. It was completed by Francesco della Luna in 1445. The building rises above a little staircase and is decorated in the vanes by nine harmonious arcades resting on slim columns in glazed earthenware by Andrea della Robbia which carry figures of putti (1463). Under the loggia are frescos by Poccetti, while the fresco with the *Eternal Father with the Innocent Martyrs*, in the lunette of the left door, is by Giovanni Francesco (1485). - The interior of the hospital, has a beautiful porch courtyard with a glazed earthenware (at the left, in the lunette) by Andrea della Robbia representing *Annunciation*. From here, through a corridor at the right, we have access into the interesting Gallery, which is made up of five halls which contain various works of art, among which the *Adoration of the Magi* by Domenico Ghirlandaio. This work made for the church of the hospital; we note also a *Madonna with Child and Angels* by Botticelli and also works by Piero di Cosimo, Giovanni del Biondo; Neri di Bicci. Sculptures by Luca della Robbia, among which the very beautiful *Madonna*. Frescos by Bernardino Poccetti and various portraits of benefactors of the institution.

CHURCH OF SS. ANNUNZIATA

It is the famous Florentine basilica which contains the venerated image of the Madonna Annunziata. Erected about 1250 by seven founders of the Order of the Servants of Mary, it was then rebuilt in 1444 by Michelozzo and retouched in the XVII and XVIII centuries. It is preceded by a porch with seven arcades built in 1601 by Giovanni Caccini with the exception of the central arch which has a fresco by Pontormo with *Charity and Faith*. This work is of an earlier date and is attributed to Antonio da Sangallo the Elder. In the lunette above the central door is a mosaic with the Annunciation by Davide Ghirlandaio (1509).

From the porch we enter a gracious hall called the CHIOSTRINO DEI VOTI, built in 1447 by Manetti after a design by Michelozzo. Interesting are the frescos that decorate the lunettes under the porch which, beginning from the right of the door represent: the

Church of SS. Annunziata.

Assumption by Giovanni Battista Rosso (1517); *Visitation,* by Pontormo (1516); *Wedding of the Virgin* by Franciabigio (1513); the relief with the *Madonna* is by Michelozzo; *Birth of Mary,* one of the most famous works by Andrea del Sarto (1514); *Arrival of the Magi* also by Andrea del Sarto (1513). *Christmas Scene* by Alessio Baldovinetti (1462), the oldest of all the frescos here made; *Vocation of Saint Filippo Benizzi* by Cosimo Rosselli (1476); then follow others with episodes of the life of Saint Filippo, by Andrea del Sarto. At the wall is a *Bust of Andrea del Sarto* by Caccini (1606).
THE INTERLOR, of famous Baroque appearance, has only one nave with profound lateral chapels and a chiselled roof with decorated stuccos. Left of the entrance is the marble little temple erected by Lapo Portigiani after a design by Michelozzo (1448), which covers the rich altar which preserves a miraculous veiled image of the *Annunciation,* a modest work of the Florentine School of the fourteenth century and which legend attributes to a thirteenth century painter, a certain Bartholomew who fell asleep and, on waking up, found the head of the Madonna completed by an Angel. The beautiful lamps, chandeliers, the silver altar are gifts of the Grand Dukes of the Medici family. In the first left chapel, *Trinity, Maries and Saint Jerome* by Perugino and helpers. In the chapel of the *Crucifix,* in the left cross-vault is a statue in terracotta of *Saint John the Baptist* by Michelozzo. Through a corridor at the right, we enter the sacresty of Lapo Portigiani after a design by Michelozzo. Round church: the frescos in the dome with the *Crowning* of the *Virgin* are by Volterrano. At the left, is a tomb of *Bishop Angelo Marzi Medici* by Francesco da Sangallo (1546). On the floor is a tombal slab by Andrea del Sarto. Behind the chorus, the central chapel called « del Sossorso » was adapted by Giambologna to contain his body and that of Flemish artists deceased in Florence. The *Crucifix* on the altar and the bronze bas-reliefs with *Stories of Passion* are by Giambologna. In the chapel at the left of this one the Resurrection is the work of Agnolo Bronzino and the wooden *Statue of San Rocco* is by Norimberga Viet Stoss, Right of the Rotonda (round church) is the *Tomb of Donato dell'Antella* by G .B. Foggini. In the fifth chapel at the right is a *Monument to Orlando de' Medici* by Bernardo Rossellino (1456). In the fourth chapel

is a sculpture group in marble of *Pietà*, by Baccio Bandinelli who is buried here. From the left transept, through a door opposite the sacresty, we enter the CLOISTER OF THE DECEASED. The door, from the side of the cloister, is surmounted by a lunette with a fresco depicting the *Madonna del Sacco*, considered one of Andrea del Sarto's best. The walls under the porch of the cloister are entirely decorated with frescos which celebrate episodes of the life of the Orders of the Servants of Mary, many of which made by Bernardino Pocetti. Through a door under the porch, one can enter the CHAPEL OF SAN LUCA, headquarters of the Company of Florentine Artists since 1562. Among the various artists here are buried Benvenuto Cellini, Franciabigio, and Pontormo.

ARCHAEOLOGICAL MUSEUM

(The entrance is at No. 9 of SS. Annunziata square, at the corner of Via della Colonna).

It has its headquarters in the Crocetta Palace and it is one of the best and most interesting archeological museums in Italy. It is made up of three sections: Topographical Museum of Etruria, Egyptian Museum and an Etruscan, Greek-Roman Antiquarium.

At the ground floor the first halls are occupied by Greek-Roman sculptures, among which of special interest are: *A little Satyr Looking at His Tail*, the Roman copy of a bronze original of the II century B.C.; *A Satyr with Dionisium as a Child*, a copy of the Roman period of a Hellenistic original; a large *Statue of Aphrodite;* a large statue of *Cariatide; Artemis Laphria*, from a Greek original of the V century B.C.; *Apollo and Apollino Milani*, Attic sculptures of the VI and V centuries B.C.; a *Lion in Val Vidone*, an Etruscan work of the IV-III century B.C. - Then follow the halls of the TOPOGRAPHICAL MUSEUM OF ETRURIA, formed with archeological objects of all Etruscan people, and ordered topographically according to territories of the various centres of Etruria in its evolution from the VIII to the I century B.C. The entrance of each hall shows an explicative placard which illustrates the material. The most important documented localities are: Tarquinia (rooms 12-14), where of special interest is the *fictile cinerary* with a bronze covering; *sarcophagi* of the IV century B.C. - Tuscania (rooms (15-16), *fictile sarcophagi* of the III-II century B.C. - Orvieto (room 18), *Funeral Head of a Warrior* of the V century B.C. - Vulci (room 19); *Funeral Lion* of the V century B.C. - Vetulonia (romms 25-28), objects originating from tombs of the VII-VI centuries B.C. - Populonia (romms 29-31), a bronze *Fibula* with a small *Venus*. - Chiusi (rooms 39-46), *Cinerary Statue* representing a mother and child and known as the Goddess Mother of the Etruscans, of the V century B.C. - Luni (room 49), decorative frontons in terracotta of two temples dedicated to the Capitoline Triad and to Apollo and Diane, of the II century B.C. - In the garden is the reconstruction with material originating from monuments of various kinds, and tombs, (Etruscan tombs above all). - Rooms 50-51 are dedicated to the section of prehistory.

EGYPTIAN MUSEUM. — It goes back to the year 1824 and is the richest in Italy after that of Turin. It is made up of objects originating from excavations made in Egypt and in Nubia, after an expedition guided by Ippolito Rossellini and from material originating from private collections. In the first eight halls of the first floor are sculptures, sarcophagi, mummies, goldsmith's shops, etc. Of particular interest are: a fragment of a group in granite with *Goddess Hator in the Semblance of a Cow Giving Milk to Pharaoh Harembeb* (XIV century B.C.); *Bust of a Pharaoh* (XVIII century B.C.); a polychrome relief with *Goddess Hator Offering Her Hand to Pharaoh Sethos* (XII century B.C.) ; two polychrome little statues of a *Girl Preparing Beer* and of *Another Handling Flour* (2625-2475 B.C.); an *Old Cart* in wood and bone, found in a tomb of a necropolis of Tebe of the XIV century B.C.

ETRUSCAN-GREEK-ROMAN ANTIQUARIUM. — It contains objects which were part of the collections of the Medici and the Lorenas and which was later increased by donations and purchases. It is composed of sculptures and bronzes. Of exceptional interest are the *Sarcophagus of Ramta Uzenai*, of the IV century B.C.; *Minerva in Arezzo, Chimera from Arezzo*, Etruscan art of the V century B.C.; *Arringatore*, an honorary statue of the Etruscan personage Aulo Metello, of the III-II century B.C.; *Idolino*, a Greek original of the V century B.C.; *Head of a Horse* of the Hellenistic period from which Donatello got inspiration for the horse of the monument to Gattamelata in Padua. On the same floor are the Mumismatic Cabinet and the collection of Jewelry such as gems, cameos, silver objects, etc. - At the second floor continue the halls belonging to the Etruscan section, with ancient things of northern and southern Italy, of Cyprus, Creta, Grece, and Rhodes. A rich collection of Attic vases and black figures of the VI century B.C. among which the famous Francois vase, a masterpiece of attic ceramics with scenes of Greek mythology, and signed by the pot maker Ergotimos and by the painter Klitias; Etruscan painting of the tombs of Vulci, Tarquinia and Chiusi; a polychrome sarcophagus by Larthia Seianti, of the III-II century B.C.

Along the right flank of the archeological museum, runs the rectilinear Via della Colonna. On the right, cornering with Via della Pergola, is the House of Benvenuto Cellini in which the great goldsmith and sculptor modelled and created his famous Perseus, placed under the Loggia of the Signoria. - Further on at No. 7 of Via della Colonna, has its headquarters the Convent of Santa Maria Maddalena de' Pazzi with the great fresco by Perugino. The street ends leading into Azeglio Square, a very vast square ornamented with gardens. On the right, in Farini Street No. 6 rises the SYNAGOGUE, erected in 1872-74 after a project of architects Mariano Falcini, Marco Treves and Vincenzo Micheli by virtue of a sum left by David Levi to the University of Israel. Oriental in style, it has a beautiful dome which is entirely covered with copper and the windows are exquisitely designed. - Via Farini leads into Via dei Pilastri from where at the left we arrive to the church of Saint Ambrose, in the homonymous square.

Convent of Santa Maria Maddalena de' Pazzi. — (Via della Colonna N. 7; if closed please ring for the guard). In the capitolar hall of the ancient convent is the famous fresco by Perugino (1493-96) depicting the *Crucifixion*, a beautiful composition divided into three parts separated by three arches: at the centre is the Crucifix with the Magdalen in Prayer; at the left, the Madonna and Saint Bernard; at the right, Saint John and Saint Benedict. A stupendous landscape acts as background for the harmonious composition.

Church of Saint Ambrose. — Erected in 1296, it was later retouched. The interior, with only one nave, has beautiful altars of the Renaissance period with paintings of the XIV-XV centuries. In the Chapel of the Miracle, at the left of the Presbitery. is a beautiful tabernacle by Mino da Fiesole (1481) and a fresco by Cosimo Rosselli at the wall with the *Procession* (1486); at the following wall, is a painting with *Angels and Saint* by Alessandro Baldovinetti. On the floor, a slab indicates where was buried Mino da Fiesole. In this church were buried other bold artists among whom Andrea del Verrocchio, Simone del Pollaiuolo called Cronaca and Francesco Granacci.

Piazza San Firenze and the Bargello Palace.

SIXTH ITINERARY

PIAZZA DEL DUOMO - VIA DEL PROCONSOLO - DANTE'S HOME - PIAZZA SANTA CROCE (CHURCH OF SANTA CROCE; PAZZI CHAPEL; MUSEUM OF THE OPERA OF SANTA CROCE) - HORNE MUSEUM - BARDINI MUSEUM.

Via del Proconsolo. — It is one of the most ancient streets in Florence beginning at the right of the apse of the cathedral. After walking along the first portion which contains the small square of Santa Maria del Campo with the homonymous church at N.o 12, cornering with borgo degli Albizi, is the so-called NONFINITO PALACE begun in 1593 by Bernardo Buontalenti upon Alessandro Strozzi's commission, and then continued by G.B. Caccini and also by Matteo Nigetti and others, but never brought to comple-

NATIONAL MUSEUM. - **Michelangelo:** Bacchus.

tion. At the present time the Palace is the headquarters of the ANTHROPOLOGICAL AND ETHNOLOGICAL MUSEUM. This museum which was founded by Paolo Mantegàzza contains collections pertaining to the various human races and to pre-history and a documentation of African civilizations as well as those of Asia, Indonesia, Oceania and of America. At the other corner at N.o 10 is the Renaissance-styled PAZZI-QUARATESI PALACE, with two floors and with splendid mullioned windows, built by Giuliano da Maiano (1642-72) for the Pazzi family.

Further ahead, on the right, is the Via Dante Alighieri which leads to a picturesque corner where in former times existed the ALIGHIERI'S HOMES: they are at present much restored. At the corner is the so-called DANTE'S HOME in which the great Poet is supposed to have been born. Continuing along Via del Proconsolo on the right we see the church of Badia and further ahead, on the left, the Bargello Palace, headquarters of the National Museum. We arrive thus at Piazza San Firenze.

Piazza San Firenze. — It is a suggestive, typically Florentine square with the 16th century Old Palace as a background on one side and on the other the beautiful view of the Bargello Palace rising severely as a fort with its 13th century tower. To this building contrasts the slim bell-tower of the church of Badia sided by the farthest outline of the Brunelleschian dome of the cathedral. On the west side is the great GONDI PALACE, one of the best examples of Florentine Renaissance, built by Giuliano da Sangallo in 1494, which the very beautiful arcaded courtyard. On the opposite side is the complex Baroque building, from which is named the square: consisting of a palace and two churches on the sides. This building with a 18th century facade is today the headquarters of the Tribunal; formerly it was the Convent of the Filippini. The church at the left is dedicated to San Firenze.

THE BARGELLO PALACE

It is so called because towards the end od the XVI century the Captain of Justice (called Bargello) came to live here with the Judges of Rota. The construction of the austere building started in 1254. At first it was the residence of the Captain of the People and later of the Podestà. It is the most important civile building after the Old Palace. It has a typically Medieval appearance with its tower called « la Volognana » standing there proud and watchful as a sentinel.

The front portion with the tower is the most ancient and is atttributed to the same friar-architects of Santa Maria Novella: Fathers Sisto and Ristoro. The back portion was built between 1260 and 1346 and to its construction took par the architects Neri di Fioravante and Benci di Cione, to whom are attributed the court-yard and the wonderful hall of the Consiglio. When the Captain of Justice took possession of the palace (together with the Judges of Rota), it was transformed into a prison and there took place the execution of the condemned. The Weapon Room was the torture place and the scaffold was in the court-yard. The instruments of torture and the scaffold were burnt by request of Grand-duke Leopoldo in 1782.

THE NATIONAL MUSEUM

It has had its headquarters in the Bargello Palace since 1859 and is of unique interest for the knowledge of Tuscan sculpture from the XIV to the XVII century.

GROUND FLOOR - ROOM I. It is divided into two parts by massive pillars. Alongside its walls are remains of the Medici armoury of the XVI-XVII century. Or particular interest are the two fire mouths; one with the head of Saint Paul and the other called Falcone: both were cast by Cosimo Cenni in the first half of the XVII century. Among the numerous armories special attention deserves the one with the figures of Abundance and Neptune, called the weapon of Charles V, a probable work of the Milanese craftsmen of the XVI century. - ROOM II (of the tower). In this hall are also found armouries of the Medici period, war trophies and a precious saddle embroided in gold and silver, of the XVII century.

COURT-YARD - Irregular in the disposition of the various architectural elements, it is rich in suggestive charm on account of the harmony deriving from and for the crowding of the images suggested by its very history. On three sides the court-yard is surrounded by an arcade under which are arranged statues by artists of the 16th century in Florence. Worthy of attention are the *Sepulchral Statue of Mario Nari, Temperance,* and *Juno,* works of Bartolomeo Ammannati; also the *Ocean* and *Virtue stepping on Vice* by Giambologna; also the *Fisherman* a statue in bronze by the modern sculptor Vincenzo Gemito. On the side, by the imposing staircase, the work of Neri di Fioravante, an airy open gallery completes the very beautiful scenery. Along the walls and under the arcades are coats-of-arms of the Podestà, of the Judges of Rota and polychrome embles of the citizens' quarters add to the picturesque qualities.

ROOM III - (Dedicated to the sculptures of the Tuscan School of the 14th century). In the centre of the hall we see a wooden support for the holy water stoup of the school of Nicola Pisano (XIII century). At the right wall is a *Madonna and Child* by the Senese artist Tino di Camaino (XIV c.); also we see another *Madonna and Her Child* in alabaster of the Venetian School of the XV century. At the back wall is an imposing statue of the *Madonna between Saint Peter and Saint Paul* by Paolo di Maestro Giovanni.

ROOM IV - Here are works by Michelangelo. The great artist is here present with his *Bacco and the little satyr,* a work of 1497 when he was a young man. The tondo of the *Madonna Who teaches how to read to Little Jesus and Saint Giovannini* (1504); the *Bust of Brutus* (1540) and an unfinished bas-relief of the *Martyrdom of Saint Andrew* are also in this hall. The *Bust of Michelangelo* is by Daniele da Volterra. At the left wall are statues and bronze works of Ammannati, of Tribolo, of Danti, and other followers of Michelangelo.

FIRST FLOOR - From the court-yard staircase at the beginning of which we see sitting on the pillar *Marzocco,* the symbolic lion of Republican Florence, we reach the balcony. Here are gathered the various sculptures of Giambologna among which the very agile and famous *Mercurio* in bronze and the naturalistic representations of animals.

THE GREAT ROOM (1) - This great hall of very beautiful architecture, called also of the General Council, contains the sculptures of Donatello, the great maestro of the 15th century in Florence. He was the one who, in the new interpretation of reality, brought to art the breath of naturalistic, human version and created in

NATIONAL MUSEUM. — The Courtyard.

the bas-relief a narrative which is solved by means of the « stiacciato » with pictorial as well as plastic effects. At the back wall is the sculpture of *Saint George* (1416) which seems to dominate the hall; this work was at one time in the tabernacle of the Armaioli in Orsanmichele - it is now substituted with a copy. At the sides are the *Bust of Giovanni Antonio da Narni*, the *Bust of Niccolo da Uzzano*, in coloured terracotta, and the bas-relief of the Crucifiction. By Donatello are moreover: the famous *David* as a young man in bronze (1430) and the other *David* in marble placed before the former; the two *Saint John the Baptist*, one the early and the other the late work of the artist; the *Marzocco* (lion with the coat-of-arms of Florence) and the famous *Athys*, the baby with the tail of a little faun which controls the rythm of the music: a real masterpiece of freshness and cheerfulness. The other works exposed in the hall belong to sculptures of the 15th century in Florence all more or less under the

NATIONAL MUSEUM. — **Donatello:** « Saint George ».

Donatello: Cupid.

Donatello: « Marzocco
the lion of Florence

NATIONAL MUSEUM. — Wedding Chest (15th century). Detail.

influence of Donatello, among whom Desiderio da Settignano with *Bust of Saint Giovannino;* Lorenzo Ghiberti and Brunelleschi, with the two famous reliefs with the *Sacrifice of Isaae* which the two artists executed in 1402, as the theme for the contest for the execution of the door of the Baptistery. The prize was won by Ghiberti. Under the influence of Donatello were also Agostino di Duccio with the multi-colored stucco representing the *Madonna with Child and Angels;* Luca della Robbia with two *Madonnas* in glazed earthenware, with the relief in bronze of the battle.

NATIONAL MUSEUM. — **B. Ammannati:** « Leda with the Swan ».

NATIONAL MUSEUM. - **Michelangelo:** Madonna and Child with John the Baptist.

ROOM OF THE TOWER (II) - Here are exposed embroidered textiles, rugs and wooden statues of the XIV-XV centuries.

ROOM OF THE PODESTÀ (III) - Here are preserved numerous enamel-works and cristal vases of Oriental, Venetian and French art of the XVI century which to the part of the collection of the Frenchman Garrand who gave them to the city of Florence in 1883. It is interesting to note in the windows at the beginning and at the end of the hall the collection of enamel works of the XI-XIV centuries.

CHAPEL OF THE PODESTÀ (IV) - Here those condemned to death spent in prayer the last hours of their lives. At the walls are frescoes attributed to Giotto representing: *Hell* on the entrance wall; Stories of the *Life of the Magdalen, of Santa Maria Egiziaca and of the Baptist* on the side walls; *Paradise,* on the wall facing the entrance where one can also see Dante's portrait. The wooden stalls along the walls and the central lectern are by Bernardo della Checca who made them for the church of San Miniato about the end of the 15th century.

ROOM OF THE OBJECTS (VI) - Here are contained very precious and rare objects which constitute one of the richest ivory collections existing today. Here are also wooden statues of Tuscan art of the XIV-XV centuries.

ROOM OF SACRED GOLDEN OBJECTS jVII) - Here are exposed various sacred objects of the XV century: chalices, monstrances, thuribles and finely chiseled reliquaries originating from Florentine churches. To be noted also is the Bust of Saint Ignatius, an example of Florentine art of the XV century.

ROOM OF THE MAJOLICAE (VIII) - Here are preserved samples of the ancient Italian factories of Urbino, Pesaro, Faenza and Florence and a few pieces of Moorish art from the fabric of Valencia of the XV century. Of importance is the beautiful grotesque painting which Orazio Fontana created for Guidobaldo II, the Duke of Urbino.

SECOND FLOOR - CELLINI'S ROOM - It is so called because here are gathered various masterpieces of the Florentine maestro, an inimitable sculptor. Let us note a *Bust in bronze of Cosimo I,* two little sketches, one in wax and the other in bronze, for the Perseus which is in the Loggia della Signoria; *Perseus liberating Andromeda;* a greyhound: a very fine relief; *Ganymede raped by the eagle;* a wax portrait of the *Grand-duke Francis I* which was by the latter sent to his second wife Bianca Cappello with a letter here exposed with her portrait. The statues in marble at the centre of the hall, also by Cellini, originate from the Boboli garden. The glazed earthenwares at the walls are from the school of Della Robbia, among which a few are by Giovanni della Robbia, the last of this family of artists.

ROOM OF THE DELLA ROBBIA (II) - Here are preserved glazed earthenwares by Andrea, Luca and Giovanni della Robbia and of Santi Buglioni.

VERROCCHIO'S ROOM (III) - Here are contained the works of this Florentine maestro (Andrea de' Cioni, 1435-88), in whose workshop was formed Leonardo da Vinci. Among the works that are exposed we note: *David,* a work in bronze of a lively rythmic appearance and of harmonious shape; a *Woman's bust with a bouquet of flowers* of a lively character and great composing harmony; two Madonnas, one in marble and the other in terracotta; a *bust of Piero di Lorenzo de' Medici;* the *death of Francesca Pitti Tornabuoni,* in bas-relief. In this hall are also works of other sculptors such as Antonio Rossellino Laurana and Matteo Cividali.

BADIA. - On the left, **Mino da Fiesole:** Tomb of Ugo, Count of Tuscany; on the right, **Filippino Lippi:** « Apparition of the Virgin to Saint Bernard ».

Two small rooms (IV-V), expose the Medici medal show-case, with samples which were made during the Renaissance period and attributed to Pisanello, Matteo de' Pasti, Michelozzo, Cellini, L. Leoni.

ROOM OF THE CHIMNEY (VI) - It takes the name from the chimney originating from the Borgherini Palace and sculptured by Benedetto da Rovezzano (XVI century). Here are also works of 16th and 17th century sculptors: *Bacchus* and a *Faun* by Iacopo Sansovino; the *Bust of Costanza Bonarelli* by Lorenzo Bernini; a bronze chandelier with the Medici weapons and coat-of-arm by Valerio Cioli, and another chandelier with the insignia of the Guelf Side, of Tuscan art of the XVI century.

ROOM OF THE SMALL BRONZE WORKS (VII) - It contains a very beautiful collection of money, medals, plates and little bronze statues of the Renaissance period by Ghiberti, Antonio del Pollaiuolo, Tacca, M. Soldani, Giambologna, by whom are the *Fatigues of Hercules*, a few *Venuses*, and the little sketch for the famous Mercury.

Badia. — It is an ancient Benedictine church founded in the X century by the Countess Will, the mother of the Marquis Ugo of Tuscany. In 1285 the church was enlarged and from that period remains the external flank. Finally, it was retouched in the XVII century by Matteo Segaloni who transformed the interior in Baroque forms. The rich portal, surmounted by a lunette in terracotta with the *Madonna and Child* by Benedetto Buglioni (XV century) is the work of Benedetto da Rovezzano (1495), the author of the interal porch which acts as a vestibule for the church. From the extremity of the porch is visible the slender hexagonal bell-tower of the XIV century which is constituted by two styles: Romanesque at the botton and Giotto at the top.
The interior is shaped like a Greek cross with a very beautiful attic of Baroque style by Felice Gamberai and Domenico Dotti after a design by Matteo Segaloni (1625). Here are also found works of the Tuscan Renaissance. At the right is the *tomb of Giannozzo Pandolfini*, from the workshop of Bernardo Rossellino;

near-by is the *Madonna and Her Child and Saints Lawrence and Leonard,* a bas-relief for altar frontal by Mino da Fiesole (1464-69). In the right arm is the *tomb of Bernardo Giugni* by Mino da Fiesole (1468). In the left arm is the tomb of *Count Hugo the Marquis of Tuscany;* this finely decorated masterpiece is by Mino da Fiesole. Above is the *Assumption,* by Giorgio Vasari. Then follows a chapel with frescos representing *Scenes of the Passion* of a Giottesque character but which tradition attributes to Buonamico called Buffalmacco. On the entrance wall is a board with the *Apparition of the Madonna to Saint Bernard,* a valuable work by Filippo Lippi (1480). From the choir, through a right door, one goes up to the 15th century CLOISTER OF THE ORANGE TREES with two orders of columns sustained by columns with interesting frescoes in the upper arcade with *Stories of Saint Benedict,* attributed to the Portoguese Giovanni Consalvo.
Opposite the church of Badia starts Via Ghibellina which is flanked, at the beginning and on the right, by the left side of the Bargello Palace No. 70 is Buonarroti's home.

Buonarroti's Home. — Bought by Michelangelo, his heirs transformed it into a museum in honour of the great ancestor. It is interesting, for here are preserved the early works of Michelangelo which are gathered in the hall of the first floor. Among these works are the high-relief of the *Battle of the Centaurs and Lapithae* of 1429, and the *Madonna and Child* also called the Madonna of Saint Lawrence. In the same hall is also the portrait of Michelangelo, a bust in bronze by Daniele da Volterra. The adjacent hall exposes a collection of drawings: studies of of the nude, compositions, portraits, as well as architectural projects. In other halls are *Portraits of Michelangelo,* one by Bugiardini and the other by Venusti; a *Portrait of Vittoria Colonna,* the woman loved by Michelangelo, attributed to Pontormo. At the ground are found the drawings of the works of Michelangelo preserved outside of Florence: the *Prigioni* in the Louvres; the Madonna in Bruges; the Moses in Saint Peter in Vincoli, Rome; the Pietà Ronadanini in Milan, and others.

Almost opposite Buonarroti's home is Via delle Pinzochere which leads directly into Piazza Santa Croce.

Piazza Santa Croce. — It is the square which has followed the evolution of the customs of its city: from the first gatherings of the people who listened to the voice of the preachers of the faith of Christ, to the fifteenth-century merry-go-rounds of the knights, among which the one won by Giuliano de' Medici and made immortal by the verses of Poliziano, to the 16th-century soccer disputes to which participated enthousiastically the Florentine people. In rectangular shape and with the church of Santa Croce as background, it is surrounded by ancient palaces, among which at No. 1 is the COCCHI SERRISTORI PALACE, built in 1470 by Baccio d'Agnolo; at No. 21 is the PALACE OF ANTELLA, built by Giulio Parigi in 1619 with its multi-colored facade: the frescos were completed in only 27 days by 12 painters under the direction of Giovanni da San Giovanni.

CHURCH OF SANTA CROCE

It is one of the most renowned Franciscan churches in Italy. The construction of the building was begun in the second half of the XII century and completed at the end of the XIV century. It is a masterpieçe of the Gothic-flo-

Church of Santa Croce.

rentine architecture attributed to the genius of Arnolfo di Cambio, the same architect of the Signoria Palace and of the Cathedral. The marble facade is the modern work of Niccolo' Matas (1857-63). The *Madonna* above the central portal and the *Triumph of the Cross* in the underlying lunette, are by Giovanni Dupré, The *Finding of the Cross* in the lunette of the left portal is by Tito Sarrocchi; the *Vision of Constantine* in the lunette of the right portal is by Zocchi. The beautiful bell-tower, which is of Gothic style is the work of Gaetano Baccani (1865).

In this church, since ancient times, wanted to be buried those Florentines who were attracted by the new and profound preachings of the Order that advocated humility, poverty, chastity against the opposing customs of the period. Thus. little by little, the church became a great cemetery. Members of noble Florentine families and personalities of that time found here in great number eternal rest. Funeral monumets, tombal slabs and memorial plaques in ever-increasing number were built. These gave

CHURCH OF SANTA CROCE. — Interior.

to the temple the characteristics of a sanctuary of the citizens' memories. It became later a national reliquary as famous men in every field were buried there, and even if not all were buried, funeral monuments were erected to testify a spiritual presence.

THE INTERIOR. — It is shaped like an Egyptian cross and is divided into three naves by elegant pillars and pointed arches. The attic, as in all Franciscan churches, is covered with open-truss roof. At one time the walls were entirely decorated with frescoes by Giotto which could have lasted to our days were it not for Giorgio Vasari who, after the order of Cosimo I who wanted the church restored, had them plastered and put by the walls altars of scarce importance.
Beginning from the internal wall of the facade we note the *Monument to Historian Gino Capponi* by A. Bertone (1884) and the *Monument to the poet G.B. Niccolini* by Pio Fedi (1883). At the third pillar, right of the median nave, is a very beautiful marble pulpit by Benedetto da Maiano, with Stories of Saint Francis (1476).

RIGHT NAVE. — At the first pillar is the rythmic and exquisite bas-relief with the *Madonna del Latte* by Antonio Rossellino (1478). Opposite, at the wall, is the *Tomb of Michelangelo* by by Giorgio Vasari (1564). Past the second altar is the *Cenotaph in honour of Dante Alighieri* (buried in Ravenna), by Stefano Ricci (1830). Past the third altar is a *Monument to Vittorio Alfieri* by Canova (1810), of pure neoclassical style. Past the IV altar is a *Monument to the Historian and Politician Niccolò Machiavelli* by Innocenzo Spinazzi (1787). Left of the fifth altar is the *Tomb of Historian Luigi Lanzi,* by Giuseppe Belli (1810). Then follows the very beautiful Renaissance tabernacle in clear stone with the the relief of the *Annunciation,* a masterpiece by Donatello (1435). After the delicate door leading into the cloister, is the very beautiful *Tomb of the Humanist and Chancellor of the Florentine Republic Leonardo Bruni,* the work of Bernardo Rossellino (middle of the XV century), a prototype of Florentine tombs of the Renaissance; then follows the *Tomb of Gioacchino Rossini,* by Giuseppe Cassioli (1886). The corpse of the musician who died in 1868 was transported here

SANTA CROCE (Sacristy). - **Taddeo Gaddi:** Crucifixion.

Paris in 1886. After the last altar, is the *Sepulchre of the Poet Ugo Foscolo,* whose corpse was brought here in 1936, with a statue by Antonio Berti (1939).

RIGHT TRANSEPT. — At the right is the CASTELLANI CHAPEL decorated with the interesting cycle of fourteenth century frescoes representing at the right *Stories of Saint Nicholas from Bari and of the Baptist,* and at the left, *Stories of Saint John the Evangelist and of Sant'Antonio Abate,* by Agnolo Gaddi, Gherardo Starnina and others. At the back wall is a Crucifix on a board by Niccolò Gerini (1386). The statues at the pillars of *Saint Francis* and *Saint Dominic* are in terracotta and by the Della Robbias. In the transept is the BARONCELLI CHAPEL with the cycle of frescoes representing the *Stories of the Virgin,* a masterwork by Taddeo Gaddi (1338); on the altar is a polyptych with the *Coronation of the Virgin,* with Giotto's signature; at the back wall is a *Madonna della Cintola with Saint Thomas* by Sebastiano Mainardi (1490). At the exterior of the chapel, on the right, is the *Tomb of the Baroncellis* attributed to the Senese artist Giovanni di Balduccio (XIV century). - Through the door that follows, by Michelozzo, one enters the barrel-vaulted corridor with elegant windows. From the door at the left we can go into the sacresty of fourteenth century architecture, decorated with frescoes by Niccolò di Pietro Gerini (end of the XIV century) with *Stories of the Passion.* In the very beautiful cupboards by Giovanni di Michele (1454) and Nanni Ungaro (1530), are precious corals in mi-

SANTA CROCE. - **Giotto:** Death of Saint Francis.

SANTA CROCE. - **Giotto:** Vision of Fra' Agostino.

SANTA CROCE. - Tomb of Michelangelo.

niature, sacred vestments and the relics of Saint Francis. In the back wall, closed by a Gothic gate, is the RINUCCINI CHAPEL, with frescos by Giovanni da Milano and his helpers, representing the *Stories of Mary Magdalen of the Virgin* (1366) and a polyptych on the altar with a *Madonna and Saints*, by Giovanni del Biondo (1379). Returning to the corridor, on the back is the MEDICI CHAPEL (or the Noviziato Chapel), built by Michelozzo in 1434, with a beautiful tabernacle by Mino da Fiesole (1474), a bas-relief attributed to Donatello and on the altar is a *Madonna and Child and Saints*, a glazed earthenware by Andrea della Robbia (1480).

BACK CHAPELS. — At the sides of the major chapel are aligned five chapels, each built in part by the best Florentine families whose name they take, and dedicated to the Saint Protector of the family. Beginning from the extreme right the first is the VELLUTI CHAPEL which later passed to the Morelli and Riccardi families, with remains of frescos attributed to a pupil of Cimabue, representing the *Stories of Saint Michael the Archangel*. The second is the BELLACCI CHAPEL, frescoed by Taddeo Gaddi, it was restored in the XVII century by Gherardo Silvani. The third is the *Chapel of the Silvestri Family*, then Bonaparte, with the *Monument to Carlotta Bonaparte* by Lorenzo Bartolini. The fourth is the PERUZZI CHAPEL and is very important because of Giotto's frescos made around 1320 and then covered by plaster and later badly restored in the XIX century. At the right wall are *Stories of Saint John the Evangelist*. From above is: *Vision in the island of Patmos*; *the Saint resuscitates Drusiana*; *the Saint goes to Heaven*. At the left wall is *Stories of Saint John the Baptist*. From above: *Annunciation of the Angel to Zachariah*; *Birth of the Baptist; Banquet of Herode and Salome who presents the Head of the Baptist to Herodias*. At the sides of the window are four Saints and in the vault, the symbols of the *Evangelists*. The fifth, right of the major chapel, is the BARDI CHAPEL *which* is also decorated with Giotto's frescos with the beautiful *Stories of Saint Francis* which were found in 1853 and not damaged by the most recent restorations. At the exterior of the chapel is *Saint Francis receiving the Stigmata*, and, in two medallions *Adam* and *Eve*; in the archivault are eight busts of Saints; at the left wall, from above: *Refusal of the Inheritance; also Apparition in the church of Arles to Saint Anthony who is preaching; Death of the Saint*. At the right wall, from above is the *Approval of the Rule, Test of the Fire before the Sultan; Visions of Friar Agostino and the Bishop Guido*. In the vault: allegories of *Poverty, Obedience, Chastity*, and *Saint Elisabeth; Santa Clara*. The board on the altar wall of the window: *San Lodovico of Saint Francis and Stories of His Life*, of the end of the XIII century, is attributed to Barone Berlinghieri, a painter from Lucca. The MAYOR CHAPEL' or Alberti Chapel, contains frescos by Agnolo Gaddi with the *Legend of the Cross* (1380). A fresh, live, dynamic narration: the prototype of the Florentine-gothic painting. On the altar is a polyptych with the the *Madonna and Child*, by Niccolò Gerini; at the sides, is the *Four Doctors of the Church*, by Nardo di Cione; above the altar, is a *Crucifix*, a painting of the School of Giotto. The seventh left of the major chapel, is the TOSINGHI CHAPEL (later Spinelli and Sloane), frescoed by Giotto at one time with the *Stories of the Virgin*, of which remains only the *Assumption* on the external arch. On the altar is the *Madonna and Saints*. a polyptych by Giovanni del Biondo (1372). The eighth is the CAPPONI CHAPEL, dedicated to the Italian mother, with the *Piety* of Sculptor Libero Andreotti (1926), here placed after the first world war. The ninth is the RICASOLI CHAPEL, with frescos and paintings by Luigi Sabatelli and his sons Giuseppe and Francesco (XIX). The tenth, is the PULCI CHAPEL (later Berardi and Bardi), with frescos by Bernardo Daddi (1330), the one who was able to combine the mo-

SANTA CROCE. - Pazzi Chapel.

numental character of Giotto's painting with the Gothic of the Senese (with the help of his pupils); the frescos represent the *Martyrdom of Saint Lawrence and Saint Stephen.* On the altar is a shovel in glazed earthenware by Giovanni della Robbia, with a *Madonna and Child and Saints.* The eleventh is the CHAPEL BARDI DI VERNIO with frescos representing *Stories of Saint Silvester,* by the favorite disciple of Giotto, Maso di Banco, called little Giotto. At the altar is *Saint John Gualberto and Stories of His Life,* by Iacopo di Cione (end of the XIV century). The NICCOLINI CHAPEL, the last of the transept, was architecd by G. B. Dosio and is dedicated to the Assumption of the Virgin. Rich of XVI-XVII century decorations, it has the vaults frescoed by Baldassare Franceschini, called Volterrano (1660). Then follows the BARDI CHAPEL with the famous *Crucifix* in wood by Donatello (1425). This chapel was criticized by Brunelleschi for its excessive realism and thus he wanted to design, to support his criticism, the also famous Crucifix which is located in the Church of Santa Maria Novella. At the following is the SALVIATI CHAPEL, with the beautiful *tomb of Princess Sofia Zamoysky*, by Lorenzo Bartolini (1837). LEFT NAVE - Between the sixth altar and the door is the *Tomb of Carlo Marsuppini* (a humanist), a magnificent work by Desiderio da Settignano (1460), who got inspiration from the opposite monument by his maestro Rossellino. At the fifth altar, on the floor, is the *Tombal Slab of the Tomb of Galileo Galei*, by G. B. Foggini and G. Ticciati (1737). At the wall are remains of fourteenth century frescoes.

THE PAZZI CHAPEL

The entrance is on the right of the Church of Santa Croce and it leads into the evocative fourteenth century cloister where on the left looks out the arcaded flank of the church. In the background rises in all its harmony and balanced grace the Renaissance jewel of the Pazzi Cha-

MUSEUM OF SANTA CROCE. - **Andrea Orcagna:** The Poor invoking death.

Cimabue's Crucifixion which was destroyed by the flood of November 4th, 1966.

pel by the genius of Brunelleschi who worked at it from 1430 to 1446.

The exterior with its elegant porch, has the frieze formed by heads of cherubs by Desiderio da Settignano. The porch has at its centre a small hemispheric dome with decorations in terracotta by Luca della Robbia. By him also is the *Saint Andrew* above the engraved door, by Giuliano da Maino (1472). The interior, in rectangular plan, is of remarkable simplicity with the typical Brunelleschian decoration in clear stone on white plaster. The only things in colour are the frieze which has a decoration in glazed earthenware by Luca della Robbia; the medallions high in the walls and in the pendentives of the dome with the *Apostles*, they also are in terracotta by Luca della Robbia; we also see the glass windows of the apse with *Saint Andreffi* after a design by Alessio Baldovinetti. Right of the chapel, a portal leads into the imposing and simple second cloister which is also by Brunelleschi.

Museum of the Opera of Santa Croce. — The entrance is from under the porch of the entrance cloister and is placed in the old refectory of the convent. The vast place is ornated with frescos by Taddeo Gaddi, among which *The last Supper* which occupies a whole wall. Reordered in 1959, the museum contains paintings of the fourteenth and sixteenth century, sculptures and architectural elements belonging to the church. To be noted is the *San Lodovico from Tolosa*, a sculpture in gilded bronze by Donatello (1425); a very beautiful *Crucifix*, by Cimabue; *Saint John the Baptist* and *Saint Francis*, a fresco by Domenico Veneziano (1455); the *Triumph of Death and Hell*, remains of frescos by Andrea Orcagna originating from the church; a *Madonna*, by Bernardo Daddi. In addition to the above, there are also sculptures by Tino di Camaino and other important works by various artists of the XIV-XV-XVI centuries.
Once we have completed the visit to Santa Croce, it is convenient to take on the left Magliabechi Street which on the left flanks the building of the CENTRAL NATIONAL LIBRARY the entrance of which is from Cavalleggeri Square No. 1. The construction of this imposing building of modern style with some Renaissance characteristics, is due to the Architect Cesare Bazzani (1911-35). This library is the most important in Italy and enjoys international reputation. Magliabechi Street leads into the Avenue of Tintori, where by turning right at the end at the left cornering with Via dei Benci, rises the ALRERTI AND CORSI PALACE, attributed to Giuliano da Sangallo. In this palace was born Leon Battista Alberti, one of the most famous architects in the Renaissance. Beautiful indeed is the internal couryard built by Giuliano da Sangallo with the collaboration of Andrea Sansovino. The palace is the headquarters of the Horne Foundation to which we have access from Via dei Benci No. 6.

Horne Museum. — It was founded by the English Art Herbert Percy Horne who had bought the palace. At his death, which happened in 1916, he donated to the city of Florence the palace and the precious collection. In the museum are collected ancient objects, paintings, sculptures, collections of precious objects, souvenirs, furniture, rugs of value, etc. Of special interest, at the ground floor is the front part of a large case of the fifteenth century with Paris lying down and the painting with the *Adoration of the Child*, by Lorenzo di Credi. In the three halls of the first floor, is a *Madonna and Child* and a *Pietà* by Simone Martini; *Deposition* by Benozzo Gozzoli; *Saints*, by Sassetta; *Allegory of Music* by Dosso Dossi; *Saint Jerome* by Bernardo Daddi; *Ester*, by Filippino Lippi; *Saint Stephen*, a painting attributed to Giotto. Among the sculptures: a *Wooden Statue of San Paolo*, by Vecchietta and a *Bust of San Giovannino* from the School of Desiderio da Settignano. The halls of the second floor contain the collections of drawings, the library and various objects of art.

The Bardini Museum. — It was given to the city of Florence in 1923 by the Florentine Antique Collector Stefano Bardini. The curious palace, interesting on account of its windows formed with original architectures of altars coming from a church in Pistoia, contains in twenty halls a rich collection of Etruscan, Greek, Roman, and XIV-XV century sculptures; also valuable paintings, rugs, arrases and Renaissance furniture. Of special interest is an *Archaic Etruscan Sepulchral Pillar* of the II century B.C.; a fragmentary altar with Bacchus and Maenad, of Greek art of the VI century; *Charity*, a statue attributed to Tino di Camaino; footings of the altar, by Michelozzo; reredos of the altar by Andrea della Robbia; a statue in terracotta of the Madonna of Senese art of the XV century. Among the paintings of special interest is the *Crucifix* attributed to Bernardo Daddi and *Saint John the Baptist* by Michele Gianbono.

SEVENTH ITINERARY

VIALE DEI COLLI - PIAZZALE MICHELANGELO - CHURCH OF SAN MINIATO AL MONTE - VIA SAN LEONARDO - FORTE BELVEDERE.

Viale dei Colli. — After a visit to the museum, the churches and monuments and works of art of which Florence is rich, it is indispensable to take a ride along the Avenue of Colli. This avenue, which sums up the natural and artistic beauties of the city and its environment, besides being the most beautiful in Florence, is also one of the most famous roads in Italy. This avenue is about 6 kilometers long, goes up the hill at the southern end of the city and begins from Francesco Ferrucci Square. The first part; namely the one that goes up to Piazzale Michelangelo is called the Avenue of Michelangelo and offers magnificent green scenery and panoramic views.

PIAZZALE MICHELANGELO

It is the most suggestive part of the famous walk along the Viale dei Colli. From the balcony one can enjoy an almost complete view of the panorama of the city, which is divided into two parts by the Arno river, and of the surrounding hills.

In the background at the left we can see the large green area of the Cascine Park; and, looking towards the right, we see the three tops of Mount Morello, then the hills of Careggi, Montughi and Pratolino. Almost opposite, past the valley in which we can see Mount Senario, the hills of Fiesole with the bell tower of the cathedral in the middle are visible to us.
Further on the right is Mount Ceceri and soon after the castles of Poggio Gherardo, Vincigliata, Poggio, and finally the hill of Settignano. Stupendous indeed is the view of the city below with all its monuments rising above houses as in a dream. At the extreme left of the flank of the Arno we see the bell tower of Santo Spirito and the characteristic dome of the church of Cestello; carrying our glance towards the right, on the other side of the Arno, in the background rises the bell tower of Palazzo Vecchio; then rises the great mass of the cathedral with the dome by Brunelleschi and Giotto's bell tower. Left of this we see the upper part of the Baptistery; in the background is the dome of the Medici chapels of Saint Lawrence; nearer is the bell tower of the church of Badia and the tower of the Bargello; further on the right is the bell tower of the near church of Santa Croce; at a greater distance is the dome of the Synagogue. Along the Arno are visible, on the left, the bridge of the Grazie, Ponte Vecchio, the bridge of Santa Trinita, the bridge of Carraia, the bridge Amerigo Vespucci and, in the distance, the bridge of Victory; on the right, is the bridge of San Niccolò. The massive construction beneath the balcony is the door of San Niccolò built in 1324 after a desing by Andrea Orcagna, which was part of a fortified point of the ancient walls of the city. At the centre of the square rises a monument dedicated to Michelangelo, with a synthesis of the most renowned sculptural works of the incomparable artist: the David is at the centre and around the pedestal, are the four statues which adorn the Medici sepulchres in the chapel of Saint Lawrence (1875). This marvelous appendix to Florentine beauties is the work of Architect Giuseppe Poggi who thought of and created it in 1869. At the other extremity of the square, at the wall preceded by a little garden, is a big epigraph which is conceived in this way: « Giuseppe Poggi a Florentine Architect - turn around - this is his monument ».

Behind the square of Michelangelo, almost hidden among cypress trees, rises the church of San Salvatore of the Mountain, which can be reached on foot by means of the staircase at the beginning of Galileo Avenue, or by automobile after having gone along the first part of the avenue as far as, on the left, a balcony can be seen: at this point begins an asphalted road which goes up as far as the church of San Miniato.

San Salvatore al Monte. — Built in 1475 after a desing by Simone del Pollaiolo called Cronaca, it was called by Michelangelo « the beautiful country girl » on account of its grace. This was the last work of the great Florentine Architect. In Renaissance model, the interior is austere and simple with only one nave, and a rectangular apse. At the altars, are a few paintings of the XV century.

A view of Florence from Piazzale Michelangelo. ▶

Continuing to go up the asphalted avenues flanked by meadows, we arrive at the church of San Miniato which rises high above a hill.

CHURCH OF SAN MINIATO

It is preceded by a vast square from which we enjoy a beautiful view of the city and of the surrounding hills. It was begun in the XI century and ended in the XIII century. It is a construction which, with the Baptistery, constitutes a rare sample of Romanesque-Florentine architecture. In the upper portion of the typical facade covered with white and green marbles, built in 1062, we note a mosaic by an unknown author of the XII century with *Christ between the Madonna and Saint Miniato*: when the sun rises its golden portion sends out sparkling rays. The fronton is surmounted by a gilded copper eagle, a symbol of the corporation of the Art of Calimala (merchants of wool).

CHURCH OF SAN MINIATO. - **Michelozzo:** The Chapel of the Crucifix.

Church of San Miniato.

The interior is made up of three naves divided by columns. In the central nave the marble floor is marked with signs of the Zodiac, and lions and pigeons (1207). At the walls of the lateral naves are visible remains of frescos of the XIV century. In the back of the median nave rises the gracious tabernacle of the first part of the Renaissance, called CHAPEL OF THE CRUCIFIX and erected by Michelozzo (1448). The work was sponsored by Piero de' Medici called Gottoso in order to preserve the miraculous Crucifix of Saint John Gualberto which is now found in the church of Santa Trinita. The vault of the tabernacle is in terracotta by Luca della Robbia, while the paintings of the little doors with *San Miniato and San Giovanni Gualberto, Annunciation and Stories of the Passion,* are by Agnolo Gaddi (1394). Behind the tabernacle is the very vast crypt in seven naves over small columns (XI century), closed by a beautiful iron gate built in 1338. From the right nave a staircase leads to the Presbytery which occupies the part above the crypt. At the wall of the nave is a fresco with a *Madonna and Few Saints* by Paolo Schiavo (1426). The Presbitery is closed by a very beautiful transenne on which rests the pulpit, built in 1207: it is one of the most notable works of Romanesque-Florentine sculpture. Behind the transenne, is a wooden choir of 1466. The Crucifix on the high altar of the XII century in terracotta and by the della Robbias. In the semicircular apse are columns and arches in black marble below and above are long windows with slabs of pink alabaster. The mosaic in the bowl of the apse represents *Christ between Mary and Saint Miniato* of the year 1297. - Right of the Presbitery a door leads inside the SACRESTY (1387) which has its walls entirely frescoed by Spinello Aretino with sixteen *Episodes of Saint Benedict's Life;* the benches along the walls are of the XV century. Returning to the Presbitery, trough a staircase at the left we go down to the left nave where are the chapel of Saint Iacopo also called CHAPEL OF THE CARDINAL OF PORTUGAL. It was architected by Antonio Manetti the pupil of Brunelleschi (1459-66), on invitation of King Alfonso of Portugal for the burial of his nephew Iacopo of Lusitania, the Archbishop of Lisbon, who died

in Florence in 1459. The five medallions in the chapel vault represent *Cardinal Virtues* and the *Holy Ghost;* they are by Luca della Robbia (1461-66); in the big niche at the right is the *Tomb of the Cardinal of Portugal,* the work of Antonio Rossellino (1459-61); in the back niche the two winged angels in fresco, are by Antonio del Pollaiolo, while the painting on the altar with *Saints Vincent, James and Eustachius,* is a copy of a painting by Antonio and Piero del Pollaiolo preserved in the Uffizi Gallery; in the left niche, above the Bishop's Chair, is the *Annunciation* by Alessio Baldovinetti (1466-67). At the end of the left nave in the church is a *Tombal Monument to the Poet Giuseppe Giusti* with an epigraph dictated by Gino Capponi.
At the right of the church rises the laced PALACE OF THE BISHOPS, built in 1295 as a summer residence for Florentine Bishops. The bell tower, built by Baccio d'Agnolo in the first half of the XVI century, was of great help the artillery during the siege of Florence (1527-30). The technical direction of the fortifications for the defense of the city in this sector was given to Michelangelo who improvised the fortress in the zone where now is the monumental cemetery called « Porte Sante » (Holy Doors), to which we go from the right of the vast square.

Viale Galileo. — It is with this name that the Avenue of Colli continues from Piazzale Michelangelo. Almost a plain, it unwinds itself flanked by big plane-trees. On the left we see little villas surrounded with gardens, little woods and cypress trees; on the right, it is a continuous succession of romantic views over the underlying farms and in the background of magnificent panoramic parts of the city. Almost at the end of the avenue which leads into the vast Galileo Square, on the right is San Leonardo Street which leads to Forte Belvedere. Right of Galileo Square begins Machiavelli Avenue which is the last portion of the promenade of Viale dei Colli. This avenue, flanked by Gardens, orchards, and villas, goes down (in a serpentine way) as far as Porta Romana Square. Here ends the promenade of Viale dei Colli. After Porta Romana, the street of the same name leads to the centre of the city.

Via San Leonardo. — It is one of the most picturesque and tipical country roads in the neighbourhood of Florence. Very narrow, it is often flanked by walls from which we see olive branches and picturesque villas. About the middle, on the right, rises the monumental Romanesque little church of SAN LEONARDO IN ARCETRI, which contains a marble pulpit of the XIII century and a few paintings of the Tuscan School of the XIV century. Before arriving at the end of the street which leads to San Giorgio's Gate, of 1324, at the left, we can enter Forte Belvedere.

Forte Belvedere. — It was erected by Giovanni de' Medici and Bernardo Buontalenti in 1590-95. The whole is formed by a central building and imposing glacises from which we have a magnificent panoramic view of the city. In the little palace of the fort is a DISPLAY OF DETACHED FRESCOS, originating from various localities and mape up of works of great value, among which the *Deluge,* the *Sacrifice of Noah* by Paolo Uccello; the *Annunciation* by Botticelli; a *Saint Jerome* by Piero della Francesca; *Stories of Saint Benedict* by the so-called maestro of the cloister of Oranges. In addition there are works by Taddeo Gaddi, Maso di Banco, Andrea Orcagna and others.

 The Church of San Miniato seen from Forte Belvedere. ▶

CENACOLO (SUPPER-ROOM) OF FOLIGNO

(42, Via Faenza)

It is the ancient refectory of the ex convent of Saint Onofrio, decorated with a fresco depicting « The Last Supper » brought out into light in 1845. The work is of the Umbrian-tuscan school of the XVI century and is attributed to Perugino. The ex convent contains the Ferroni Gallery with paintings by Lorenzo Monaco, Filippino Lippi, Carlo Dolci, Luca Giordano and other artists of various schools from the XV to the XVIII century.

CENACOLO (SUPPER-ROOM) OF SAN SALVI

(16, Via Andréa del Sarto)

In the ancient refectory of the ex abbey of San Salvi is the famous fresco depicting the « Last Supper » made in 1519 by Andrea del Sarto. It is one of the masterpieces of XVI century painting.

MUSEO STIBBERT

The Stibbert Museum is in the Montughi quarters, From Via Vittorio Emanuele, after having passed Villa Fabbricotti, the « International Students' House », we go up towards the Museum. The villa where this Museum has its seat has been built in the medieval style by Frederic Stibbert. This florentine citizen, son of an English father and Italian mother, learned conoisseur of art and enthusiastic collector of artistic objects and antiquities, succeded in putting together a collection of arms and harnasses which, in importance, can compete with the famous collection of arms in Turin.
He placed his precious collection his villa and, after his death in 1906, he left the villa together with the whole collection to the Commune of Florence. The communal administration, in 1911, named the street after Frederic Stibbert, and the Villa was then arranged as Museum.
We here find valuable objects of general use and householdware, forniture, ceramics, porcelain, tapestries, sculpture, paintings arranged in the various rooms, as well as parts of costumes of different periods and from many countries.
Of particular interest are the armours, and most suggestive is the CAVALCADE of 6 completely armed riders in natural size, which has been arranged in room VIII; in room IX we can see beautiful armour of the 15th century.
We find in this Museum Napoleon's regalia which he wore on the occasion of his coronation as King of Italy.

STIBBERT MUSEUM. — The « Cavalcade » of Knights in Italian and German Armour of the 16th century.

The hill of Fiesole as seen from San Domenico.

Panorama of Fiesole from San Francesco.

FIESOLE

This ancient Etruscan city is the most often visited place in the suburbs of Florence. It enjoys a very beautiful geographical position over a hill (295 meters above sea level) from which our glance can contain the whole Florentine valley.

San Domenico di Fiesole. — This pleasing village is found half way between Florence and Fiesole and takes this name from the convent which was built at the beginning of the XV century.

◀ The Badia of Fiesole.

The church, with its facade retouched in the XVII century by Matteo Nigetti, contains in the interior valuable paintings among which one with the *Madonna and Child and Saints*, by Beato Angelico who lived here before transferring to the convent of Saint Mark; a Crucifix of the school of Botticelli and works by Lorenzo di Credi, Sogliani and others. - In the capitolar hall of the convent, is a Crucifix, by Angelico (1440).

Left of the church, at about 5 minutes walk, is the CHURCH OF THE BADIA FIESOLANA which was the cathedral of Fiesole until 1028. In 1466 it was rebuilt, together with the convent, in Brunelleschian forms while keeping incorporated in the primitive Renaissance facade left unfinished the ancient Romanesque prospect with white and green marbles.
The interior is beautiful and harmonious. In the refectory of the convent, is a fresco with *Christ served by the Angels* by Giovanni da San Giovanni (1629).

Taking the road towards Fiesole, we reach the main square of the ancient town.

Mino da Fiesole Square. — It occupies the place of the ancient Forum and the centre of the town. Opposite rise (northern side)the Cathedral; on the left is the BISHOP SEMINARY; in the background is the Pretorio Palace, now the Comunale, of the XIV century with the facade adorned with coats of arms of the Podestà; at the right is the ancient oratory of Santa Maria Primerana (restored) with the facade of the XVII century and containing frescos of the XIV century and other valuable works of art. South of the square ,opposite the City Hall, rises the Equestrian monument depicting the meeting of *Victor Emanuel II and Garibaldi at Teano*, the work of Oreste Calzolari (1906).

The Cathedral. — Dedicated to San Romolo, it was begun in 1028 and enlarged later in 1256 and 1300. The facade and the sides, of admirable simplicity, are all made of stone. The characteristic bell tower with the great clock is of the year 1213. The interior with a truss roof has three naves divided by columns originating from pagan temples and with the presbytery located above the crypt. On the major altar, is a polyptich with the *Madonna with Child and Saints* by Neri di Bicci; in the semi-basin of the apse, is a fresco with the *stories of San Romolo*, by Nicodemo Ferrucci. Right of the presbytery, is the Salutati chapel with frescos by Cosimo Rosselli of the XV century. Here is also the sculptural masterpiece of Mino di Giovanni da Poppi called Mino da Fiesole who had sculptured the very beautiful *Sepulchre of Bishop Leonardo Salutati;* the bust of the bishop and the back of the altar with a *Madonna and Saints* (1464). The altar and the statues of San Romolo and San Matteo, in the chapel left of the presbytery, are works of Andrea Ferrucci (1493).

Roman Theatre. The entrance into the archaeological zone is behind the apse of the Cathedral. We see right away the FAESULANUM MUSEUM which contains for the most part objects collected in the excavations of the territory of Fiesole. Etruscan tombs, fragments of architectural decorations, Etruscan and Latin inscriptions, bronzes, coins and objects of the barbarian and medieval periods. Of special interest in the second hall is the small Etruscan-ionic statue depicting *Hercules* and the Etruscan mirror with the *Sacrifice of Polissena*. In the third hall is the *Head of the Statue of Claudius*.
The theatre, typically Greek, was discovered in 1809 and excavated in 1873. It goes back to the time of Silla, but in the I and III century A.D. it was beautified and enriched; it still preserves the auditorium with three orders of seats and 19 steps. Near the

FIESOLE. - Roman Amphitheatre.

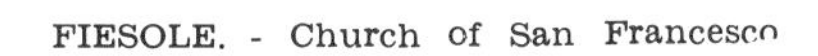

FIESOLE. - Church of San Francesco

FIESOLE. - Terrace of Saint Francis.

Theatre are visible the *Terme,* also of the epoch of Silla. A little road towards the West, leads to the Etruscan-roman *temple;* at the right we observe the remains of an Etruscan door with remains of the Etruscan Walls.

Bandini Museum. — It contains very beautified terracottas by the della Robbias of the XV and XVI centuries and furniture of the XIV and XV centuries. Moreover, here are also other important paintings by Ambrogio Lorenzetti; Iacopo del Sellaio; Neri di Bicci, Nardo di Cione, etc.

Saint Francis. — We reach it by going along the little road leading steeply down to the church of Saint Francis, rising on top of the hill. From the terrace, which takes the name of the church we can enjoy the wonderful and stupendous view of Florence and surroundings. The church in Gothic style, preserves in the interior valuable works of painters. In the convent, of interest are the gracious little cloister and the Missionario Museum.

SAN FRANCESCO. - Cloister of San Bernardino.

SAN FRANCESCO. - **C. Rosselli**: Adoration of the Magi.

CERTOSA DEL GALLUZZO (or of Val d'Ema)

From Senese Street, which begins from Porta Romana, crossing the town of Galluzzo, we arrive at the Certosa which rises out of cypress and olive trees like an ancient castle, dominating the underlying valley in which the Greve and Ema rivers come together. It was founded in 1341 by the Florentine Niccolò Acciaioli (1310-65), the great seneschal of the kingdom of Naples and the Viceroy of Puglia.

After going op the big staircase, we reach the two halls which contain an interesting collection of works of the XIV and XV centuries and five frescos (in very bad shape) made by Pontormo, hich were found at the beginning in the large cloister; they depict, *Prayer in the Orchard, Christ before Pilate, Christ Falls under the Cross, Deposition and Resurrection.* The Church, dedicated to San Lorenzo, faces a large square and has a beautiful facade in Baroque style by Giovanni Fancelli by whom are also several decorative sculptures (second half of the XVI century). The interior is in Gothic style with cross vaults and is divided according to the rite of Certosa; namely, into two parts one for the monks and one for the lay-brothers. The decoration of the place is of the XVIII century, while the paintings of the Florentine school at the altars are of the XVI and XVII centuries. From the choir of lay-brothers we go into the CHAPEL OF SANTA MARIA OF THE XVI CENTURY with very beautiful stalls of carved choir of ogival style of the first half of the XV century. At the the walls, are paintings of the Florentine school of the XIV century and on the altar is a beautiful painting of the CROWNING OF THE VIRGIN, by Alessandro Allori. From here we go down to the underground chapels of incomparable beauty. In the CHAPEL OF SAN TOBIA, left of the major altar, we find the Gothic *arch of Niccolò Acciaioli* of the end of the XIV century and on the floor are three tombal stones of the Acciaioli family. At the right is the entrance into the CHAPEL OF SAINT ANDREW, which has in the floor the beautiful *tomb of Cardinal Agnolo Acciaioli,* attributed to Donatello but more probably made by one of his followers (1409). Returning into the chapel of Santa Maria, through the corridor we reach the monks' choir located in the back part of the church. This choir contains 36 wooden stalls made after a design of Cosimo Feltrini, works of sculpture of maestros from Carrara of the XVI century and frescos by Poccetti in the Presbyterium.

In a visit to the convent the following are of greatest interest: the PARLOUR with its interesting glass windows by Giovanni da Udine (1560) and terracottas by the Della Robbias; the LITTLE CLOISTER, of the sixteenth century; the REFECTORY with a XV century pulpit; THE HALL OF THE CAPITOL, in which is kept the very beautiful fresco of the *Crucifixion* by Mariotto Albertinelli (1505) and the *tombal slab of Bishop Leonardo Buonafedi* with the figure of the deceased, the work of Francesco da Sangallo (1545); the BIG CLOISTER decorated with 66 medallions by Andrea and Giovanni della Robbia depicting *Adam and Eve, Jesus, Saints, Prophets and Sybils.* From here we pass to visit an example of a prison of the monks from Certosa. The CLOISTER OF THE CONVERTED follows and is of the XV century of Brunelleschian style and the vast guest-room in which used to stay great personalities among whom Pius VI in 1798 before the forced exile and Pius VII, the prisoner of Napoleon (1809).

TIMETABLE OF MUSEUMS AND GALLERIES

STATE MUSEUM : opening hours

Summer : 9,30-16,30
Winter : 9,30-16
week days

	Entrance fee	Hours and fee holidays	Closed on
Galleria degli Uffizi Loggiato degli Uffizi, 6	L. 250	9,30-16 L. 125	Monday
Galleria Palatina Piazza Pitti, Palazzo Pitti	L. 200	9,30-16	Tuesday
Museo degli Argenti Piazza Pitti, Palazzo Pitti	—	9-13 L. 100	Tuesday
Appartamenti Monumentali Piazza Pitti, Palazzo Pitti	—	9-13	Tuesday
Galleria d'Arte Moderna Piazza Pitti, Palazzo Pitti	L. 150	9-13 L. 150	Tuesday
Galleria dell'Accademia Via Ricasoli, 52	L. 150	9-13 L. 75	Monday
Museo Nazionale (Bargello) Via del Proconsolo, 4	L. 150	9-13 L. 75	Tuesday
Museo di San Marco Piazza San Marco	L. 150	9-13 L. 75	Monday
Museo della Casa Fiorentina Antica - Piazza Davanzati, Palazzo Davanzati	L. 150	9-13 L. 75	—
Museo Archeologico Piazza SS. Annunziata, 9	L. 150	9-13 L. 100	—
Casa Buonarroti Via Ghibellina, 70	L. 100	9-13 L. 100	Tuesday
Opificio delle Pietre Dure Via degli Alfani, 78 Saturdays 9,30-12,30. Saturday and Sunday 9,30-16,30	L. 100	9,30-12,30 L. 50	
Cappelle Medicee (Tombe di Michelangelo) Piazza Madonna Summer: 9-17 Winter: 9-16	L. 160	9,30-12,30 L. 80	—
Giardino di Boboli Piazza Pitti Summer: 9-18,30 Winter: 9-16,30	—	Free	—

Museo della Fondazione Horne Via dei Benci, 6 — Open on Mondays and Thursdays Entrance fee L. 100.

Ring the bell for visiting the following:

	Entrance fee	Entrance fee holidays
Cenacolo di Andrea del Sarto a San Salvi - Via A. del Sarto, 16	L. 100 *	L. 50
Cenacolo di Santa Apollonia Via XXVII Aprile, 1	free	free

	Entrance fee	Entrance fee holidays
Cenacolo del Conservatorio di Foligno - Via Faenza, 42	free	free
Cenacolo del Ghirlandaio Borgognissanti, 38	free	free
Chiostro dello Scalzo Via Cavour, 69	free	free
Crocifissione del Perugino Via della Colonna, 11 Closed on Sundays.	free	—

On Sundays free entrance to all Galleries.

MUNICIPAL MUSEUMS AND GALLERIES

Holiday time-table - 9-12
Free entrance on Sundays

	Entrance fee	TIME TABLE Summer	Winter
Palazzo Vecchio e Quartieri Monumentali - Piazza Signoria	L. 150 *	9-18	9-16
Galleria Corsi - Museo Bardini Piazza de' Mozzi	L. 100 *	9-16	9-16
« Firenze com'era » Via S. Egidio, 21	L. 100	10-16	10-16
Chiostri Monumentali di Santa Maria Novella	L. 100	9-18	9-16
Cenacolo di Santo Spirito e Fondazione Romano Piazza S. Spirito	L. 50	9-13	9-13
Museo Stibbert Via Stibbert, 26	L. 100 *	9-16	9-16

50 % reduction for groups of 10 persons and more.

OTHER MUSEUMS

Galleria Corsini - Via Parione, 11 - Open on Saturdays from 12 to 13 - Entrance free.

Galleria dello Spedale degli Innocenti - Piazza SS. Annunziata - 9-17,30 - Holidays 10-13 - Entrance fee L. 50.

Museo di Antropologia ed Etnologia - Via del Proconsolo, 12 - Open on demand - Holidays: 9,30-12,30 - Entrance fee for holidays L. 100.

Museo dell'Opera di Santa Croce - Piazza Santa Croce, 16 - 9-12; 15-18 - Entrance fee L. 100 - Holidays: 10-12 Sundays free entrance

Museo dell'Opera di Santa Maria del Fiore - Piazza Duomo, 9 - Summer: 9,30-13;; 15-18 - Winter: 10-16 - Holidays: 10-13 - Entrance fee L. 150 * - Sundays free entrance.

Museo Zoologico « La Specola » - Via Romana, 17 - Open on demand.

Museo degli Strumenti Musicali - Via degli Alfani, 84 - 10-12 - Free entrance - Closed on Sundays and holidays.

Museo Nazionale dell'Artigianato - Piazza della Libertà - 9,30-12,30 - Free entrance.

Museo Nazionale di Storia delle Scienze - Piazza dei Giudici, 1 - 9-12; 14-17 - Holidays: 10-12 - Entrance fee L. 200.

Palazzo Medici-Riccardi - Via Cavour, 1 - Summer: 9-13; 15-17,30 - Winter: 9-2 - Entrance fee L. 100 - Free on Sundays.

*** 50 % reduction for groups of 10 persons and more.**